C. J. Sleez

Poor Little Bitch Girl

A notice to all law enforcement employees and affiliates

Attention: <u>Any</u> and <u>all</u> arrest-able offences mentioned in this book are to be interpreted as creative non-fiction and <u>not</u> as actual confessions. I accept absolutely <u>no</u> responsibility for any of the illegal acts that may be discussed within these memoirs. It has <u>not</u> been my intention to endorse acts of crime or substance abuse.
– **CJ Sleez**

Manor House Publishing Inc.
452 Cottingham Crescent,
Ancaster, Ont., L9G 3V6
www.manor-house.biz
905-648-2193

C. J. Sleez

Poor Little Bitch Girl

Unapologetic memoirs
from the Queen of raunchy rock 'n' roll

Library and Archives Canada Cataloguing in Publication

Sleez, C. J., 1978-
Poor little bitch girl: unapologetic memoirs from the queen of raunchy rock 'n' roll / C.J. Sleez.

ISBN: 978-0-9736477-6-1

1. Sleez, C. J., 1978-. 2. Rock musicians--Canada--Biography. I. Title.

ML420.S632A3 2005   782.42166'092
C2005-905988-5

Copyright © 2005 by CJ Sleez, contents and lyrics
Foreword © 2005 by Michael B. Davie

All rights reserved. No part of this book may be reproduced, stored in a retrieval system, or transmitted in any form or by any means, electronic or mechanical, including photography, recording or otherwise (except brief passages for purposes of review) without prior written permission from the publisher.

Published Oct. 30, 2005, by Manor House Publishing Inc.
452 Cottingham Crescent, Ancaster, Ontario, L9G 3V6
www.manor-house.biz. 905-648-2193

Cover photo by Emira Becukic
Cover design: Michael B. Davie/Emira Becukic/CJ Sleez

All rights reserved.

First edition.

The publisher gratefully acknowledges the financial support of the Book Publishing Industry Development Program (BPIDP), Department of Canadian Heritage, the Ontario Arts Council and the Canada Council for the Arts.

Foreward

CJ Sleez. The name evokes fantasies in the minds of her male fans, with visions of the slender blonde writhing on stage to a driving rock beat punctuating songs she belts out with screaming intensity.

Her name commands respect – and in some cases, fantasies again – in the minds of female fans who would like to be more like her. If only they had the guts, the nerve, the figurative balls to risk it all on a life of touring clubs and halls to belt out songs of defiance. But any desire to trade places with this angel of darkness might lose of its lustre if her fans were more aware of the wrenching hard times this rock and roll icon has endured.

Poor Little Bitch Girl is a raw, unapologetic recounting of pain, loss and hard times. Don't look for any sugar-coating or smoothing over of difficult moments. CJ's memoirs are as hard and rough as they come.

In *Poor Little Bitch Girl*, CJ Sleez exposes her young life like an open wound, chronicling her rise to fame as a rock diva and her rapid fall into heavy drug addiction, failed relationships and brushes with hardened criminals, including one experience in which a drug dealer/associate ended up dead.

With this much pain running through her prose, it's easy to forget that this is still a young woman – in her twenties – who has already endured a lifetime of hardships, disappointments and difficulties.

Not that *Poor Little Bitch Girl* relates purely hard times. Also in these pages are recollections of memorable concerts, bizarre tour experiences, funny asides and much more. As well, we close with CJ's Songbook, a collection of lyrics inspired by her life and drawn from her recordings.

CJ Sleez takes a no-holds-barred approach to life. She's a creative force of remarkable talent and a destructive force to be reckoned with.

Poor Little Bitch Girl is a testament to an enduring free spirit. CJ states: "within these pages I have bled." Read her raw memoirs, and let her bleed — all over your mind.

- **Michael B. Davie,** president, Manor House Publishing Inc.
Author, *Poetry for the Insane: The Full Mental.*

Table of Contents

Foreword
Prologue

1. The End of the World
2. Skeletons
3. The Devil's Playground
4. The Rancid Wine
5. The Crash
6. House Party
7. Mount Hope
8. Riotstar
9. Amityville
10 The Sinisters
11 Eating Ashes
12 Club Ritz
13 69 Paradise
14 Punkfest
15 High School Hookers
16 Close Call
17 Hanrahan's
18 Unhappy Birthday
19 The Sleezmobile
20 The Elmocambo
21 Fleur Du Mal
22 Stacy Stray
23 Temptress
24 California Christmas
25 Prisoner
26 No Sleep 'till Lisbon
27 Aftermath
28 Wilhelmina Waste Case
29 Some People Just Don't Last
30 Death is Romantic

Epilogue
Lyrics

I dedicate this book to myself,

for within these pages I have bled.

Prologue

I'll spare you the many mundane details of my "typical" middle class childhood.

Instead, I'll begin my memoirs not with my birth (as tradition may dictate), but with the time that I started to look at my life with a certain objectivity.

Coincidentally, this new view of the world synchronized with my initial experimentations with what society would label as "street drugs."

Don't get me wrong, I am by no means suggesting that substance abuse instilled in me an otherwise unattainable enlightenment.

I'm merely saying that drugs were part of a place beyond parental boundaries.

I began to question every major influence in my life and re-examine my aspirations.

Suddenly, I was free to explore a side of life which until then, had been censored, disguised and denied to me.

I craved adventure with a fury of energy and youthful impatience.

Grade nine was the year that I really started exercising my independence.

I knew that it was time for the real fun to start and I was ready for it.

I was a teenager on the road to individuality.

This is where my story begins.

1.

The End of the World

I was born in the summer of 1978.

During my adolescence, I developed a less than optimistic outlook of the future.

Not only did the end of my childhood coincide with the Gulf war, but, as the millennium approached, the entire world seemed to be holding its breath in anticipation of a sudden global disaster.

Pop culture was focused on Armageddon with big blockbuster movies, books and music being released on the topic.

Y2K was causing wide spread paranoia and the prophesies of Nostrodamus were more popular and loosely translated than ever before.

My generation was among the first to be burdened with the overwhelming consequences of the environmental ignorance of every age and civilization that came before us.

So there I was, an incredibly confused teenager expected to map out my life and make the decisions that would direct my career and define my livelihood over the next few decades.

Meanwhile, the whole world was telling me it was all going to come to a screeching halt, sooner than later.

The unfortunate thing was, I believed them. I wanted to believe them.

In my eyes, the human race had evolved into an irreversible and ultimate evil.

We killed animals, our planet, and even each other.

Each breath I took was weighed with guilt because I was a part of it all.

I would have gladly sacrificed my own life if it were to be terminated during the total annihilation of all humanity.

We deserved an apocalypse and I was ready to get in line.

I made the decision to enjoy my life while I had the chance. What was the point of studying seriously or struggling to build a life, just to have it all come crashing down around me? It was time to live fast and die young.

I was twenty-one when the millennium came without so much as an earthquake.

It was devastating.

I was thoroughly disillusioned. Betrayed and sentenced to live out my years in a hateful, capitalist world. All was lost.

So here I am in 2005, and nothing's really changed.

People are predictably obsessed with watching sex, war and death on their television sets, still making all the same mistakes.

Where does that leave me?

Well, I'm still waiting for the world to end.

2
Skeletons

As a child I had very little interest in my own family history and it was never openly discussed.

It wasn't until I reached my early teens that my struggle to understand my own mental issues led me to question my heritage.

I began to wonder if maybe my insanity might be hereditary. After some intense and emotional interviews with both sides of my family, it became clear to me why my ancestry was keep so quiet all those years.

As it turned out, I am a direct descendant of a long line of addicts and lunatics.

My first visit was to my mother's parent's place.

My Grandmother confessed that, much like me, she has been plagued by bouts of serious depression for most of her life. She is extremely sensitive and has thoughts of suicide even to this day.

My Grandfather started smoking at the ripe old age of seven and was an alcoholic throughout the bulk of my childhood, although in recent years he had managed to stop drinking. I soon discovered that of all of his siblings, he was the most stable.

My Grandfather had two sisters, Genie and Imelda. Both were addicted to pills and alcohol and were kicked out of high school because of it. Even in her later years Genie was unable to keep a job. Her mind was too muddled and she lacked the ability to think clearly, or at least that's how it was explained to me by my Grandfather.

Imelda was a bi-sexual who lived in Toronto with her lesbian lover. She was known for her severe mood swings and violent temper, often threatening people with knives and other weapons. Imelda had a short-lived affair with a man and became pregnant, although he refused to recognize the child as his own.

Apparently, Imelda was so delusional, that she used to swing the infant out of her apartment window by a rope and bang it repeatedly against the side of the brick building.

This was her way of making the child tough enough to withstand the trials and tribulations of everyday life.

Thankfully the baby was swiftly taken away from her and sent to live with my Grandmother.

However, within a year the child inevitably came to love her and began calling her mother. My Grandmother was terrified that Imelda would kill her if she ever overheard this, and so the child was sent back home. When she was fifty-six years old, Imelda died of lung cancer.

Another one of the unstable characters from my mother's family history was a woman named Hazel.

She was my Grandmother's aunt and was best remembered for the big black Cadillac she drove. Hazel was a terminally lonely, childless widow who became so overcome by depression and drug addiction, that she locked herself in her garage and left the Cadillac running.

My Grandmother still recalls the night she came to say good-bye to her.

My father's side of the family was just as crazy if not more so. He was the oldest of five wild brothers. When he was in his late teens and early twenties, he spent most of his time on the road with his brother Nick. They were members of a psychedelic rock band called "The Village Stop" which was based out of Greenwich Village.

The band was renowned for their outrageous stage antics, such as covering their entire bodies with black-light paint and dancing around the bar nude. Sometimes my father would don a tattered wedding dress with nothing on underneath and flash the audience during what he felt were key moments in their set.

While the two eldest were enjoying with rock n' roll lifestyle, the other three brothers were finding plenty of fun back in Hamilton. Russ was independent, outgoing and popular. He was always the life of the party and could comfortably mix with any crowd. Peter was a rebel and as soon as he was old enough, he joined "the Red Devils" motorcycle gang. Rick was the youngest and followed Peter's lead. They started using drugs heavily and before long Peter became a full time dealer.

One day, Peter and his best friend Gator drove out to Montreal to score a bunch dope off of another biker gang.

They were sitting in a run-down strip club waiting for their connection, when a member of a rival club walked in with a machine gun and opened fire. Gator was killed instantly. Peter managed to hit the floor in the nick of time and dodge the barrage of bullets. He was lucky that time.

A few months later Peter and Ricky were at a clubhouse bash and some skank was screwing all the guys.

She was a Red Devils regular and could usually be found strutting around stoned, drunk and naked at their parties. On that particular evening though, she stayed upstairs as each of the members went up and took their turn with her. While this night wasn't much different than any other for her, somehow her father found out what she had been doing and completely lost it.

Embarrassed and ashamed, she tried to salvage what was left of her tarnished reputation by crying rape.

The entire club was immediately arrested and charged, including Peter and Rick. My father came back and bailed them out. About a week later, he spent the day with Peter.

They were hanging out having a beer and discussing the dreadful situation, when Peter casually mentioned that soon it would no longer be a problem. My father didn't think much of it at the time and Peter didn't bother to elaborate. Unfortunately though, he was dead serious.

His idea of solving their problem was to build a big bomb and blow up the girl's house.

With the assistance of a fellow member, he assembled the explosive, loaded it into the back of a van and drove it over. They parked directly in front of her house and were in the process of unloading the bomb when it accidentally went off. They never stood a chance. The worst part of this story is that when the rape case finally went to trial, it was quickly thrown out of court. With a good lawyer, several incriminating photographs and plenty of damning testimonies, the girl was proven beyond a shadow of a doubt to be a contentious lying slut and Ricky was set free.

Their father served in the British army during WWII.

He was charismatic, a heavy drinker and a proud womanizer. Shortly after divorcing from my Grandmother he decided to marry a woman half his age.

However, on the night of his bachelor party, he and his best man drove home drunk. They ended up rolling his green jaguar several times and his friend died on impact.

My Grandfather walked away with severe head wounds and permanent brain damage. After that he was never the same and his fiancée left him.

He was no longer capable of holding down a job and became increasingly paranoid and delusional.

He struggled with his injuries for a few short months before giving up entirely.

One morning, he woke up early and cleaned the whole house. He took out the trash, cut the grass and parked the car in the garage. Then my Grandfather calmly went upstairs to his bedroom, put on his uniform and shot himself in the head. Although he had left one of the second story windows slightly ajar, it took over five weeks for the neighbours to start complaining about the sickening smell that was coming from the rotting corpse.

When I asked about the earliest known history of my father's side of the family, I learned that the closest I come to having a famous relative, is that one of them was the last person to be publicly hanged in England.

His name was James Murphy and he was a notorious criminal. In 1878 he served five years in prison for housebreaking and upon his release he became a poacher.

The Police Constable was always on his case and had served him with several summonses. Murphy was continually threatening the officer's life but the policeman refused to take him seriously.

One night Murphy was hanging out in front of the local pub with his friends and the Constable thought he'd go over and hassle them. This was apparently the last straw for Murphy as he pulled out his gun and murdered the man without hesitation. Murphy was now a fugitive on-the-run.

The Inspectors assembled a search team and spent months in his pursuit. As a poacher he knew the land well and was able to continually avoid the authorities.

In his absence, an inquest was held at the Inn.

After many eyewitness testimonies, a jury consisting of the town's elders found James Murphy guilty of wilful murder and issued a warrant for his arrest.

A reward of one hundred pounds was offered for his apprehension and handbills featuring a woodcut of him as well as a full description were distributed all over England.

Hundreds of miners joined in the manhunt, but even with the assistance of bloodhounds, Murphy continued to elude them. Years passed before he was finally caught poaching on Royal property. And he was publicly hanged.

3
The Devil's Playground

Somehow I always knew I'd end up being a drug addict.

When I was ten years old and still way too young to have access to cigarettes (except for the ones that I occasionally managed to swipe from my grandparents), I resorted to smoking dried leaves, pine needles, catnip and other strange organics. I would roll up huge cigars in three ring paper, sit in a tree and smoke the horrid things.

It's not like I was doing it to look like a badass or impress anyone either because I'd do it alone. It's strange, but for whatever reason, I still prefer to get high by myself.

When I was in grade seven, a police officer came to my school and did an anti-drug presentation for all the students.

He brought with him a display board that showed examples of every kind of illegal drug (or at least fake versions of them). The potency and effects of each substance was listed below each faux sample.

The assembly was intended to freak us out and turn us away from the stuff, but all it did was fuel my appetite for the forbidden. I can remember hoping that by the time I reached twenty-five, I would have the chance to try each and every one of those drugs first-hand.

By the following year I had become the only girl ever to be suspended from that middle school. I had managed to convince my friend Paula to cut class that afternoon and take me to her house to get drunk. We walked over and raided her parent's unlocked liquor cabinet, mixing ourselves several amateur cocktails. I say amateur, as back then our drinks always contained a shot from each liquor bottle and were mixed with only a small splash of soda.

Those were the days when we had to take a small amount of everything so it would seem like nothing was missing. The point was to get smashed, not to enjoy the taste and after chocking down the first drink, the second one was always easier.

Everything was going fine that afternoon, until for some stupid reason I thought that I'd be better off taking the school bus home, than staying and having to deal with her parents. I was obviously loaded and I knew that they would bust us in a second. I slowly staggered back to school, but got nailed by one of the gym teachers while taking a short cut across the football field.

They phoned my mother and told her to come pick me up. I can't say that she was surprised.

Another way that my friends and I would get our kicks before we had access to any real drugs was to play a game that we called "out cold." The object of the game was to strangle someone until they passed out. Once unconscious, they would do all sorts of amusing things like convulse and talk gibberish. The trick was to deprive the brain of oxygen just long enough to induce an entertaining state of senselessness. I was always one of the first to volunteer and several times I came to surrounded by laughing friends with no memory of the brief event.

"Out cold" was a tribute to the frustration of being young and broke with nothing fun to do.

The first street drug I had the chance to try was cocaine.

I was still in grade eight when my fifteen year old sister offered me some. Giselle was also the first person to smoke me up. She showed me what good weed and hash should smell like so that no one would rip me off and she taught me how to brew bots. I was thankful for the knowledge and knew that I would have eventually found my own dope anyway. It's not as if she was corrupting me or anything, I was born a nonconformist.

By the time I got to high school I had developed yet another bad habit. I was a cutter. I used to slice myself up with knives, razor blades and broken glass.

I kept the scars from my new obsession a secret and for over a year I wore nothing but long sleeves (even in the summer). I became addicted to the pain, to the release of it all. Deep down I was so unhappy and angry with myself that the sting of the razor helped to externalize my suffering. Bleeding my inner demons helped to take my mind of the real agony that I was going through. It wasn't until I started getting tattooed that I eventually stopped.

I got my first tattoo when I was fifteen. It was done in a University of Toronto dorm room by some art student. I got a black ankh on my left thigh and was immediately hooked. I liked the idea of expressing myself in a permanent way.

I got my first piecing a few weeks later at an outdoor rock concert. There was a big purple bus parked near the merch booths where a couple of inept punks were doing discount piercings. They used an ear gun to force a stud through the side of my nose. It was utterly improper and unsanitary but I didn't care. I just wanted it done.

A few hours later NIN hit the stage and I made my way to the front of the mosh pit. I was doing OK until some guy who was crowd surfing kicked me in the head with his Docks and put my new piercing straight through the cartilage between my nostrils.

After that it took weeks to heal. Even back then I was fearlessly reckless. People were always surprised to see such a tiny chick battling it out at the front of the stage.

However, the few times I was knocked down, I was picked right up again. As violent and crammed as it was in there, the kids were always looking out for each other.

4
The Rancid Wine

When I was in my early teens, for whatever the debatable reason (rebellion, curiosity, boredom etc.), I became preoccupied with the idea of getting fucked up.

Some kids were into sex, I inclined towards (and still do), drugs and alcohol. However, being legally under age for cigarettes and alcohol combined with limited resources and close to no cash, it was a daunting indulgence.

My parents had stopped stalking liquor after several raids by my older sister. The only intoxicant they didn't touch was that which they considered completely undrinkable, the so-called wine in the cellar.

They knew no sane person could pour a glass and actually bring themselves to drink the foul liquid.

They were right about the "sane" part, as I've never claimed to be, but when I found that filthy room in the basement, with its walls piled high with dusty green wine-bottles, I knew that I had hit the mother lode.

The history of the rancid wine began in 1982 when my father decided to try to make his own. Problems with the batch began, when due to inexperience, he decided to store the barrels in his brother's hot garage for the summer.

After that, it was moved (along with us) into the century and a half year old mansion they still call home. As my father has never been one to waste, he stacked the murky bottles and barrels into a small room located in the far back corner of our dirt floor basement. There the spoiled liquid remained, untouched and forgotten, for the next ten years.

I can remember swiping the first bottle, pulling it out to share with a group of friends at a local bush party.

It was so strong and nasty we drank it in shots, daring each other to do so in turn. The wine smelled strangely similar to varsol and for the first few gulps we held our noses to help kill the taste. The muddy coloured alcohol didn't really fall into the category of red or white. In fact, we all agreed it was like nothing we'd ever seen before.

When I held the clear glass bottle up against the light I could see small pieces of what looked like rust floating in the fluid. It was absolutely putrid, but we kept drinking and very soon after, we were wasted. Mission accomplished.

Within a couple of weeks, I was stealing them two at a time. Although most nights I still had to thoroughly convince my pals that it wouldn't kill them, I (the constant masochist) actually grew to enjoy the taste. My peers were impressed with my ability to continually stomach the terrible solution and in high school; such ridiculous things are what reputations are built on.

However, that was never one of my main concerns, and as it turns out, I was merely in training.

To avoid raising suspicions with my increasingly frequent trips to the basement, I soon found myself stockpiling bottles in my closet six at a time.

I had access to an almost limitless supply of free booze and I was taking full advantage of it.

Despite the gut rot and recurring nausea, I was having a great time. Still, I was getting cocky and it was only a matter of time before I'd be busted by someone. As it turned out, I got caught by just about everyone.

The first incident was at a high school dance. I had never gone to one before and couldn't understand why any student would want to return to school after dismissal.

Nevertheless, in the spirit of trying everything once, one of my girlfriends managed to persuade me to accompany her. I had little faith in her promise that the dark gymnasium filled with teachers masquerading as chaperons, would be a hip place to be. In anticipation of the staggering uneventfulness, I decided to bring along a little insurance. On arrival, the scene was just as I had pictured.

The gym was scattered with groups of awkward teens, all more concerned about how they looked to each other than having fun. There was a large screen at one end of the room that was showing all the mainstream top forty music videos. A few couples swayed back and forth together while the escorts circled the room like vultures.

There were even the benches lined with the unfortunates, the unconformable sitting in a row of silence. It was just like a tacky after-school special.

As the music changed and the tempo accelerated the dance floor began to slowly fill with more insecure adolescents. My friend spotted the guy she had come to see and excused herself, leaving me standing there alone.

At least now I know I haven't been missing anything, I thought to myself. I was only in grade nine at the time, yet my entertainment standards had already outgrown that of the average high school student.

I decided to make my way to the washroom before any guys could see me and approach. At least in there I could sneak a few drinks and hopefully by the time I got back, my girlfriend would be too. As dismal as the evening's prospects were, I wasn't going to give up on the night that quickly. Besides, I knew I'd feel better after a drink.

Inside the bathroom I was bombarded by the sound of a group of giddy girls that had congregated in front of the mirror. Each one was needlessly fixing her hair and make-up while shouting childish gossip at each other.

This was definitely not my scene. I slunk briskly past them and locked myself in the end stall.

Slumping onto the toilet seat, I opened my coffin-shaped backpack and retrieved a 1L plastic bottle full of the homebrew. I must have been in there for a while, drinking in grand gulps and drawing in my small sketch book, because sure enough, some teacher was sent in to check it out. They were always watching me (with good reason I suppose).

I knew something was amiss when I heard the ladies room door creak open and suddenly the room fell silent.

There was a scurrying of feet followed by a slam and I could sense the room was empty, except for the two of us.

Her heels clicked against the linoleum as she stepped toward me. Rather than being nervous or even scared as some kids might be, I was drunk and found this far more amusing than the actual dance. Then again, I was the only kid who brought her own refreshments.

There was a knock on the stall door followed by: "Is everything OK in there?"

"Ya sure, just piss off and let me be," I replied in a drunken slur. Two more rapid knocks. I started to snicker.

"What's going on in there?"

"Nothing, now fuck off!" I snapped. The old lady stood there for a moment disputing her next course of action.

To my surprise, she entered the stall beside me and actually stood on the seat and peered over the top of the stall. I looked up and burst into laughter. I was ready to get out of there anyway so I grabbed my stuff and staggered out. The teacher struggled to keep up with me as I walked back across the hall towards the gymnasium where the dance was being held. By the time I reached it, she had managed to retrieve the principal.

After a brief discussion about my crime and the way I had been discovered, the principal declared that it would be in everyone's best interest to keep it quiet.

I was banned from school dances for the rest of the year, and the teacher was never again to invade the privacy and sanctity of a women's washroom stall.

That was the last after school function I ever attended.

And no, I don't regret missing the prom.

5
The Crash

Hanging out with me has never been considered a healthy habit.

You're almost guaranteed to be involved in some type of illegal activity and there's a pretty good chance that your life could end up being in danger.

I've learned the hard way that very few people appreciate such a reckless lifestyle and because of this, over the years I have ultimately been abandoned by each and every one of my accomplices.

My saving graces however, are that I'm creative, confident, completely fearless, loyal until the end, and I'll always show you a good time.

I'm just more than most people can take for any length of time and I have yet to meet anyone with an equally spirited rebellious streak.

As long as I can remember I've been branded as a bad influence. When I was a kid my friends were each eventually prohibited by their parents from consorting with the likes of me.

One of these former companions was a girl named Louise and we were both fourteen at the time of the crash.

Thinking back now, I'm amazed at some of the things I've managed to convince people to do over the years.

One afternoon I went over at Louise's house after school and her dad pulled up in a brand new, candy apple red convertible sports car. It was irresistible.

I turned on the infamous "CJ charm" and before I left, Louise and I had formed a plan of action for later that night.

I went home for dinner, swiped a few beers, and stashed them under the front porch before going upstairs.

I watched the clock impatiently waiting for midnight. At twelve o'clock I snuck downstairs, retrieved the beer and went down to the end of the driveway to wait for my ride.

The night began in disappointment when I saw a turquoise station wagon slowly swerve towards me and stop. I had to jump back as the car stopped in the exact spot where I had been standing.

Sure enough, Louise had wimped out on me and suddenly our impending joyride was looking less like a fun adventure and more like a boring Sunday evening drive.

Damn, I thought to myself, I should have known that she wouldn't have the guts to bring the sports car.

Despite my shattered enthusiasm, I hopped in and we crept awkwardly back onto the black road.

"What happened?" I asked half-heartedly.

"I couldn't get the keys," she lied.

"Well at least let me try driving for a while," I replied obviously annoyed.

"I can't. My parents will kill me. Let's just go visit Alexis (my usual partner in crime) and then I'll drop you back at home."

"Geez, this just gets better by the minute," I pouted, and cracked open a beer. She stared at the bottle in disapproval and I shrugged her off with a roll of my eyes. What a square. We drove the rest of the way to Alexis's house in silence. Alexis was waiting for us at the end of her street.

She said that she had gotten too paranoid hanging out in front of her house waiting for us.

Luckily her presence was enough to break the tension that had been building in the car.

While I wanted to head downtown and have some real fun, the other girls felt that we had already done enough damage and so we headed down old Jerseyville Road for a leisurely drive through the woods.

I popped in a Led Zeppelin tape and turned it up full blast. We raced down the dark road swerving back and forth across the centre line.

Louise was without a doubt the worst driver I had ever seen. Alexis made a desperate plea for a chance behind the wheel but her request (like mine) was quickly denied.

As we sped towards to the next turn the car slid sideways and I could tell that Louise had lost what little control she had. There were thick wooden posts lining the edge of the road to prevent cars from tumbling over the edge of the escarpment and we ploughed through three of these before crashing into the woods and over the side.

We fell about twenty feet before violently slamming head on into a tree. That tree was the only thing preventing the car from plummeting the entire two hundred feet down the side of the mountain.

Alexis and Louise were in shock from the impact of both the collision itself and of the airbags which had exploded in their faces (we were all seated on the front bench with me in the middle).

Smoke began to pour out from beneath the crumpled hood and I screamed for them to get out of the car, half expecting it to burst into flames around us.

Once we were safely outside of the vehicle we were able to view the damage. The car was completely destroyed.

I couldn't even imagine how they were going to hoist it out of there.

All three of us had a different reaction to the stress of the situation. I began laughing hysterically, Alexis got extremely pissed off and Louise burst into tears.

"Let's get the hell out of here," I said after taking a moment and a few deep breaths to compose myself. The girls nodded in agreement and we began the steep hike back up the mountain. I suggested we stay off the main road as the wreck would inevitably be discovered and the police would be searching for the culprits.

With adrenaline rushing through our veins we ran through the woods towards civilization, stopping to duck and hide each time a pair of headlights passed us.

I was wearing a mini-skirt that night and by the time we made it back into town my legs were a bloody mess from the shrubs and bushes.

We left Alexis at the foot of her street and finished walking what remained of the seven kilometre stretch back to my place.

I told Louise her best bet was probably to sneak back into her house and try to look innocent when her parents woke up, but she was too terrified of her father to go home.

"It wouldn't matter anyway," she sighed. "I left the keys in the car. They'll know it was me for sure."

The two of us finally made it back to my parents place just as the sun was starting to rise.

We managed to successfully sneak in undetected and my folks were none the wiser.

When we came downstairs that morning they didn't even ask me how Louise had gotten there during the night.

They were always like that with me, totally oblivious.

Back then I used to disappear for days at a time and when I'd return they wouldn't even have noticed that I was gone.

I knew we had a hard day ahead of us, so before we got on the school bus I swiped another bottle of my parent's rotten wine.

When we got to the high school there were already two police cruisers waiting for us in the parking lot.

"Are you sure that you're ready to deal with this?" I asked Louise.

She just stood there frozen, her eyes filled with fear. "Maybe you'll feel better after a drink," I suggested and we went inside and climbed up above the auditorium stage. There was a cat walk up there and it was perfect for skipping class because you could look down and see anyone that was approaching.

After an hour or two Louise finally summoned up the courage and stumbled into the office ready to take her punishment.

A few days later I was at home and there was a loud knock at the front door.

There stood Louise's dad, red faced and fuming.

My parents politely invited him in and I eavesdropped as he explained to them the whole sordid story.

Of course in his version it was entirely my fault.

It came as no big shock to me when I heard my parents laughing.

"Well, I don't know what you expect us to do," my father said. "It's not like they were stupid enough to steal one of our cars."

I had to smile. I never got punished for anything.

So Louise's dad left looking even angrier than when he had got there and Louise was added to the long list of friends that were no longer allowed to associate with me.

6
House Party

My first major rebellion against my parents took place during my grade nine school year. Gabrielle (one of my younger sisters) was born with Downs Syndrome and so everyone in the family was attending a national conference on the topic in Moncton, New Brunswick. Everyone that is, except Giselle and myself.

I'd already attended the previous year's convention and convinced my parents to leave me behind, on the condition that my Grandmother would come over to keep an eye on me. If there's one thing that every teenage kid wants, it's to throw a party without parental supervision and I planned to do just that.

My grandmother arrived early on Friday afternoon. I had some of my friends (the ones who had taken the school bus home with me) hide behind the shed in the backyard while I went inside to wait for a phone call. I had arranged for one of my girlfriends to call me at a certain time and pretend to invite me over for the weekend.

Then, rather than stay in our creepy old house alone, I was sure that my grandmother would opt to head for home.

While I was supposed to be riding my bike to my friends, in reality I was with the others hiding behind the garage waiting for her to leave. It didn't take long, as several minutes later we watched her pull out of the driveway and we let ourselves in. I know it sounds harsh, tricking my grandmother and all, but when I want something I'm not the type to let anything stand in my way.

Once inside the house, our first order of business was to raid the rancid wine cellar. I took a bunch of guys downstairs with me to help carry some booze up and by doing so; I made the location of the enormous alcohol supply common knowledge. It was just as well though, everyone at the party was too young to bring their own booze and I wasn't about to play waitress all weekend.

Even though I was a complete freak in high school (dressing and acting differently than my peers), I remained relatively popular. My social life has always been manic depressive. I go through phases of either surrounding myself with friends and admiring acquaintances or submersing myself in complete solitude.

With me, it's all or nothing. I only mention this because within hours of faking out my Grandmother, the party had swelled to over two hundred rowdy teens.

I didn't have to wait long before hearing the first inevitable Smash! I made my way towards the front of the house where I discovered some young fool had put his fist through the glass door to the porch. He was standing there dripping blood all over my parent's carpet. Just as I was about to start screaming at him, I was grabbed from behind and carried to the kitchen table by a group of guys.

On the table was an enormous glass decanter filled with wine. It was the same size as the wooden barrels in the cellar and it must have been quite a chore hauling it upstairs while being careful not to break it. I was impressed. Laughing and mock-struggling, I was then pinned down beside the giant jug. Using a clear hose from an old fish tank they had found in the basement, they stuck one end in my mouth and started siphoning the wine straight out of the bottle. Apparently I wasn't allowed to have a bad time at my own party.

A few hours later I met my next challenge when I was called outside to deal with a guy who was perched on the roof of the shed. I couldn't help but laugh when I arrived on the so-called "scene." At its highest point the building only reached twelve feet, but this loser was threatening to jump just the same. It was absurd. I would have been surprised if he had broken a leg in the short fall let alone plummet to his ultimate demise. However, anyone willing to make a complete fool of himself just for a little compassion was obviously in dire need of some attention.

Thankfully, once he realized how ridiculous he looked it was easy to get him inside for another drink. I told him to write it off as a drunken episode and reassured him that no one would remember by Monday anyway.

Even as I said the words I didn't fully believe them.

The strange thing is that a few months later the same guy had a skiing accident and ended up paralyzed from the waist down. Talk about bitter irony.

I woke up late the next day and found the house littered with unconscious adolescents. I believe it was that morning that I experienced my first real hangover. I was proud of myself and felt like I'd really accomplished something. I dragged myself down to the kitchen and was filling the coffee pot with water when I glanced out the window. Gasping, I ran outside unable to conceal my excitement.

There was already a small crowd gathering by the time I reached the backyard. Several of the guys had brought their dirt bikes and were creating their own makeshift racetrack that circled the perimeter of my parent's three acre lot.

I couldn't imagine a better way to start the day. We spent the afternoon drinking and taking turns racing the bikes while cheering each other on. There were lots of wipe-outs but thankfully no serious injuries.

As night began to fall there was an increasingly steady flow of guests arriving or returning. Among the new arrivals was a certain young boy I'd been secretly waiting for. His name was JD and I thought he was dead sexy. JD always wore a black leather jacket that smelled like the stockroom of a leather warehouse. To this day freshly cut leather remains one of my favourite scents.

JD had black hair and beaming blue eyes. Every day he'd wear tight black jeans (which believe it or not were stylish at the time), and a fitted black t-shirt that usually advertised some heavy metal band. In the summer he'd roll his cigarettes up in his sleeve just like James Dean. Totally irresistible. I thought he would have fit right in as one of "The Outsiders."

JD was also the same guy I'd shared my first French kiss with a few months earlier. I was anxious to improve upon what must have been a brutal first impression. If I recall correctly, I believe he had said that it was too sloppy.

If only that had been the case on this occasion.

We spent the next few hours staring at each other from across the large, crowded rooms while he made an appearance with his buddies and I gathered my virginal courage. I'd made the decision that this was going to be the night. The night that one way or another I'd remember for the rest of my life. I was ready to have sex, or so I thought.

My mother, being either over precautious or extremely liberal had taken me for my first pap smear six months earlier and I had been on the pill ever since.

She was obviously expecting me to have sex. In a strange way it was almost as if she was encouraging me.

As a relatively average teenage girl I had heard all the horror stories about a woman's first time. The shock aspect of these tales ranged from pregnancy, permanent venereal diseases and AIDS to gushing blood and torn flesh.

At the same time there was also plenty of pro-sex propaganda around proclaiming the ecstasy of sex and promoting it as a desirable, alluring act. I mean let's face it, our entire society is obsessed with sex (whether they want to admit it or not). It's everywhere. It's screaming at us from every billboard and calling to us from every commercial.

Anyway, it was around this age that curiosity started to get the better of me. I wanted to find out what all the fuss was about and it was JD who happened to tip the erotic scale.

It took JD a little while that evening, but he eventually came over to talk with me and after minimal effort (from either of us), we were on our way upstairs.

I opened my bedroom door and entered only to find one of my girlfriends under the covers with her boyfriend. I smiled and suggested to JD that we find another room.

Giselle was away on one of her benders so we took hers.

I can sum up my first lay in two words, awkward and uncomfortable. There was absolutely no foreplay.

This could have been blamed on inexperience, but now I wonder if maybe he was just afraid to kiss me again. I don't even think we were fully undressed. Within moments we got frustrated with trying to make it feel good, or at least I did. I was nervous as hell and he was not helping the situation (if you know what I mean). Neither of us got off and it was over as fast and unromantic as it had begun.

As soon as we were finished I thought that we must have done something wrong. Perhaps it was due to my own impatience. After that night we barley spoke.

On the third day of my open house extravaganza, my parents phoned and some drunken moron answered it.

They were so pissed off that by the time I picked up the phone they were threatening to call the cops. I still don't know if they were bluffing or if they actually did rat us out and the cops just couldn't be bothered to show up because other than a lot of yelling, nothing happened. I still had one day left to clean the house before they got home.

By Monday morning everyone was back in school, everyone except me that is. It was my much dreaded day of damage control. I woke up still partially drunk and found myself in a total disaster zone. The clock was ticking and I needed a miracle. There were also plenty of things that I had no hope of hiding, including a couple of broken windows, some serious carpet stains, a set of blown speakers and an empty wine cellar. There were broken beer bottles all over the driveway and we had torn the hell out of the yard with the dirt bikes. It was about this time that I started getting nervous. After collecting the majority of the empty wine bottles (I counted 94), I washed the dishes and scrubbed the place down as best as I could. I tidied up the bedrooms and made the beds but unfortunately I forgot to change the sheets and later found out that my parents had discovered a used condom from one of my careless friends.

Regardless of my ardent attempts at repairing the house and concealing the havoc of the weekend, I knew I had to get out of there before they got back.

I took off to Alexis's and she convinced her mother to let me stay for a few weeks under the assumption that I had been kicked out of my house. Her mother was already well aware of my unruly antics and the story wasn't a hard sell.

About a month later I was hanging out in the high school smoking section when my Mom showed up.

My two little sisters were strapped in their car seats in the back of the jeep and they were obviously happy to see me. My Mom calmly explained that everything was OK and that they weren't mad anymore. I guess they weren't really surprised. After all, I've always been pretty wild.

I only stayed at Alexis's for a few days after that and when I did go home things really had cooled down.

My parents never said a word to me about the party. That's what my adolescence was like; if I did something that disappointed them, they would give me the silent treatment. I was never grounded and I never had any kind of curfew. I did whatever I wanted and was expected to deal with the consequences on my own.

Even the discipline notices that were sent from the high school came in the mail addressed to me. It was splendid.

My grandmother on the other hand, didn't speak to me for a couple years after that, which suited me just fine.

In the end, my grade nine house party was legendary and well worth any aggravations that it may have caused me.

I mean, come on, you're only young once right?

7

Mount Hope

The weather was warming and my grade nine school year was at an end.

I had become the biggest pot-head in my age group and my friends mainly consisted of a handful of older guys who just happened to sell weed.

Not yet interested in clothes and make-up, I was still a rail thin, short-haired tomboy.

Sex was normally the last thing on my mind and none of those relationships ever progressed beyond anything platonic.

We just hung out smoking weed and talking about music. Mostly we listened to over-exposed grunge and alternative music (which was at its peak), but we also loved classic rock like Led Zeppelin, AC/DC and Pink Floyd.

I always thought it odd that none of the other girls in my grade were into music, or drugs for that matter.

A few of these guys lived in a small picket fence town called Mount Hope.

Boasting a total population of fewer than 100 residents, it was more of a survey than a city.

With so few distractions, we entertained ourselves with extra-curricular activities such as, rolling the biggest joint in the world (it took almost two packs of rolling papers and was over a foot long), puffing pails (a ridiculously bulky and inconvenient way of smoking dope involving a bucket of water and a 2L plastic pop bottle), or going for long walks.

It was on one of these walks that we discovered the hut.

Behind the quaint rows of homes and across an old dirt road, there was a forgotten forest.

One afternoon, we followed an over-grown path and carefully crossed an intersecting stream by balancing on a fallen log.

Soon we came upon a large, slanted wooden fort.

Inside, the shack was divided into two rooms.

One section had two levels similar to bunk-beds while the other part had a make-shift table and some broken lawn chairs.

No one knew who had constructed and then abandoned the place, but we instantly made it our own.

Many of my nights that summer were spent camping out and attending small bush that we held out at the hut.

It was at one of these gatherings that I experienced the best visuals I've ever had on an acid trip.

The forest was pitch black and of course, I forgot to bring a flashlight. Although, as it turned out, I didn't need one. That night I was guided through the woods by thousands of electric purple flowers.

Every tree and bush was covered in neon lights, much like the small bulbs that decorate Christmas trees. I was blown away! How was this possible?

Unfortunately, Alexis's "trip" did not include any electric flora, and after a scream and a loud SPASH, I found her waist deep in the creek.

I literally laughed until it hurt. It's not that I didn't feel sorry for her, but in my deluded state, my sympathy was quickly conquered by the hilarity of the scene.

With a concentrated effort, I finally managed to compose myself and help her to her feet.

Holding her cold, damp hand, I guided her down my illuminated path. Needless to say, it was Alexis's first and final visit to the hut.

When we reached the clearing, we said our hellos, grabbed a couple of beers and sat beside the fire so she could start to dry off.

I spent the next few hours squatting in the dirt staring straight ahead, completely engrossed in the dancing flames.

I was mesmerized.

Never before had the colours and movements of a fire seemed so vivid and alive. Before long the coals began to come to life and intertwine with each other. The fire had somehow transformed itself into a writhing mound of grey insects right before my eyes. It was truly unbelievable.

That night gave me a glimpse into a whole new world. I had seen into the darkness for the first time.

That's how it was in the beginning. The smallest, simplest things became spectacular surprises to me again.

Ordinary nights seemed full of magical possibilities.

I felt like with each dose or drug induced stupor, I was expanding my consciousness.

It was a new perspective, that's all.

As with all big teenage secrets, the whereabouts of our play-house soon became common knowledge to the entire school.

After that, it was invaded by everything and everyone that we had originally intended to escape.

It was clear the hut would no longer be exclusively ours.

By the end of the summer the broken down shack was old news and once again it was abandoned. Left cold and empty, waiting to be claimed by the next group of degenerates.

8
Riotstar

I first saw him in the newspaper.

It featured an article on teenagers with crazy hairstyles.

Among others, was a photo of a fifteen year old with a thick black devil lock (the sides and back of his head had been shaved and the entire middle section was then pulled down over his face, ending in a sharp point just below his chin). The style was perfectly impractical and appealed to me as I had recently shaved my head.

Below the picture was his name, age (the same as mine), catholic school and address. His parent's house was only blocks away from the public high school where I had been wasting the past two years, yet we had never met.

I remember clipping the photo, although, it wasn't until a chance meeting three years later, that we came to know each other intimately.

One of my friends was having a house party downtown.

I arrived in a cab to the dilapidated building which had long since been overthrown by punk rockers.

Aluminum siding stained yellow and brown from years of rot and neglect clung to the sad looking structure.

Chaotic music called to me from the street and I let myself in. Kicking aside some trash and broken beer bottles, I descended the flight of stairs to the basement.

Downstairs, the main room was dark except for a single strobe light. Several naked people contorted in front of the flashing bulb, their only accessories the bottles of alcohol and burning cigarettes in their hands.

Apparently, I had some catching up to do. I pushed through the sweaty crowd into the kitchen, where a small group was gathered around the stove smoking hot knives.

"Need a drink?" asked a boy in a black leather jacket, as he handed me a beer. He had dark spiked hair, sharp blue eyes and was wearing a dog collar. He introduced himself as Marc and although I never told him, I recognized him immediately from his photo.

He told me he sang in a band called "Riotstar" and I mentioned I was a singer as well. Just then, a nude couple came stumbling through the door towards us. Marc introduced his guitarist TR along with his date, who before finishing her next drink, went to the washroom and spent the rest of the night vomiting on herself in the bath tub.

I still had some cocaine left from the night before so I suggested that we find a more secluded place to do it.

Marc, TR and I found an empty bedroom, locked the door and made ourselves comfortable.

After snorting a round of fat lines, Marc rolled a joint (to which I added the last of the powder), and we smoked it.

Inevitably, our conversation turned to tattoos. The three of us combined had already accumulated enough ink to cover someone's entire body.

We started comparing our works of art, but lost our inhibitions and soon became a mass of kisses and caresses.

Marc looked at me and started to undo his belt. I laughed at his presumption and jokingly suggested if he required such a service, he should ask TR. To my surprise, he did. Not only that, TR continued the jest when, all in good fun, he momentarily obliged. I loved these guys!

That was the most action any of us saw that evening. Ultimately it was a night like any other except that, from that moment, the three of us formed a friendship that lasted for years.

9
Amityville

Wilma's Place was an alternative education high school that I attended for a short time in downtown Hamilton.

It was registration day and I was sitting in the lounge, when a girl that looked almost identical to me strode by.

Like me, she had a fully shaved head and was dressed head to toe in freaky black clothes. It was almost like looking into a mirror.

When classes began I made a point of seeking her out in search of a new friend. Her name was Brenda and although we'd never met before, it turned out that she was dating my friend Marc.

Incidentally, Marc had also been expelled from school and was now at Wilma's Place with us.

It was comforting to see some familiar faces and to know that I wasn't the only punk attending the school.

The rest of the students were either Spanish, black, or white wishing they were black, pregnant, or fresh out of Juvie Hall.

I became part of a small group of outsiders. We were tattooed, pierced and drawn together by our mutual hatred for the rest of the school. In total there were under a hundred "problem" teens attending the institution, all learning through correspondence.

It didn't take long for Brenda and I to fall in love and become inseparable. I had just turned seventeen and she was nineteen so it seemed only natural that we start looking for an apartment to share that was close to the school.

We found a cheap, run-down place above a dingy bar downtown.

Right across the street was the Amity (Hamilton's own version of the Salvation Army) where we could use the payphones without being harassed by the belligerent drunks downstairs. We named the place "Amityville" due to its location and our mutual love of horror films.

I got a part-time job working at a café up the street and informed my parents that I was leaving home.

To pay the rent I had arranged with the school to attend only the first half of each day and then go to work for the rest of the afternoon. Brenda was on welfare.

We were dirt poor and starving except for our bi-monthly trips to the local food bank and whatever scraps I could sneak out of the café.

At least we always had gourmet coffee to serve our frequent guests, minus the cream and sugar.

Sharing our tiny one-bedroom flat however, was worth the sacrifices. I didn't mind sleeping on the floor when Brenda's boyfriend came over or the constant hunger pains in exchange for the freedom it offered.

One girl from school who held us both in high regard was a kleptomaniac. We told her she could come hang out with us whenever she wanted providing she brought us something each time.

As a result, she stole everything for us from liquor and cigarettes to clothes and make-up.

This system proved to be extremely profitable so Brenda and I informed the rest of our usual squatters that in exchange for access to our party house and an escape from the mundane lives of living with their parents, they also had to arrive bearing gifts.

It was the equivalent of "Ass, Grass or Gas, No One Rides for Free." Some of them stole food from their folks while others brought us things like drugs or old rock n' roll records. If someone showed up empty handed they were stuck doing the dishes.

There was never a dull moment, nor any privacy at Amityville, which suited me just fine.

One afternoon, Brenda and I got completely naked and painted each other. Then we rolled ourselves across the bedroom wall smearing black and purple paint over the nicotine stains.

We couldn't afford cable or a VCR, so I drew a rather twisted picture of several stick figures participating in various acts of deviance and taped it to the black TV screen.

On the rare occasion that things did slow down and the place got quiet, we'd pass the time by throwing burning cigarette butts out the window at the drunken bum that lived outside and laugh as he gladly scrambled to retrieve them.

However, this game stopped being fun when the bottom door lock was broken and our hallway was transformed into a homeless shelter.

It seemed that we had unintentionally drawn him in. Finally, I got sick of the smell and pushed the crazy old bastard down the stairs. After that we never saw him again.

Life went on like this for close to a year.

Before long, I dropped out of high school for the last time and was fired from my job. I was told that the official reason I got canned was because I always let my friends hang out and drink free coffee. But I beg to differ. My boss was a greasy old pervert who continuously hit on me, grabbing my ass and propositioning me on a daily basis.

On one occasion he showed up drunk during one of my shifts. As soon as he saw me he ran towards me and threw me over his shoulder, whacking my head off the counter in the process and leaving me with a large bump on my skull.

His behaviour had become progressively worse over the months until I eventually told him off. The next day I showed up for work and was handed my final pay cheque.

My part of the rent was now way past due with no other source of income or savings, I started to panic.

I couldn't apply and for welfare because Brenda was already receiving social assistance under the false pretence that she was living there alone.

For the next two weeks I desperately scanned the classifieds and distributed countless resumes to no avail.

The only add I found with any promise was for exotic dancers and boasted an earning potential of up to a thousand dollars a week.

I was still only seventeen at the time, so I borrowed Brenda's ID and answered the advertisement.

A few days later I met a woman named Nicole who along with her husband managed a handful of dancers.

The deal was that for a fee they would pick me up at six o'clock and drive down to St. Catharines where we could work without requiring an expensive city license.

I was nervous but desperate. If I wanted to stay at Amityville I had to come up with some fast cash.

The first night they picked me up I had no idea what to expect. I had never set foot in a strip club before.

Little did I know that I was embarking on a career path that would end up sustaining my extravagant lifestyle for the next eight years?

I arrived at the club in a pair of over-sized high heels that I had borrowed from a girlfriend and a tattered black negligee that I had swiped from the Amity.

The house girls snickered amongst themselves doing their best to make me feel uncomfortable while working on their turf.

My ID was photocopied and then returned to me, no questions asked. I breathed a sigh of relief. I had successfully passed for my roommate.

Nicole, realizing that this was all new to me, explained the basics: "Freelancers" were girls who paid the bar to work each evening (usually twenty to forty dollars) and only made money from private dances (which cost between ten and twenty dollars a song). The benefits of freelancing included being exempt from several otherwise mandatory stage shows and having the freedom to come and go whenever you wanted.

The other option was to be on schedule. Girls that were on shift (myself included) still had to pay a bar fee, although it was usually half the amount. In addition to this, we had to be at the club by seven o'clock to sign in, commit to staying there until closing time and dance on the stage in rotation (three to six shows per night depending on how many girls were there).

The debatable advantage to being on schedule was that in addition to the money you could make doing private dances, the club also paid you a ridiculously small salary (forty to sixty dollars a night) that could be collected at the end of the week.

I was doing my best to relax and absorb all the new information when I heard the DJ announce my name.

It was my turn to hit the stage. My main objective was to get through all three songs without exposing myself as a complete rookie.

As my first song played, I tried to imagine myself alone in our bedroom. This I managed with some difficulty and before I knew it my third song was almost over.

When I glanced over at Nicole's table for encouragement, she was raising her arms frantically trying to signal to me that I should take off my tiny dress.

I had forgotten to get naked! Mistakenly, I confused her actions as trying to communicate to me some new style of dancing. I circled the stage, raising and lowering my arms in the air above my head. Soon enough I was getting strange looks from all the patrons and staff.

Then, as suddenly as it had begun, my set ended and another girl started climbing the stairs to the stage.

"Forget something?" she asked me mockingly as she slid past. Once I was back on the main floor, I caught a glimpse of myself in one of the mirrored walls. Only then did I realize that I was still fully clothed.

So much for trying to appear experienced. Sheepishly, I made my way over to where Nichole was sitting.

"What happened?" she asked with laughter in her voice.

"I guess I forgot," I giggled. "I was just trying to focus on the music and then when I saw you, I thought that maybe I was dancing wrong."

Thankfully the episode was never mentioned to me by the management and by my second show I had it all out figured out.

We headed back to Hamilton shortly after two-thirty in the morning. I was excessively drunk and had almost two hundred dollars in my pocket.

That was the most money than I'd seen for months.

Within a year, Brenda and I each had new boyfriends and we were beginning to feel cramped in our small, overcrowded space.

By then, our relationship had deteriorated into being merely best friends.

While I have always been a blatant bi-sexual, Brenda, as it turned out, was merely experimenting. In any case, I was now able to afford a place of my own. I knew it was time to move on, and so together Brenda and I made the joint decision to leave Amityville.

I still smile when I drive by that old bar. It was a time in my life that I'll never forget.

10
The Sinisters

I was slumming around downtown Hamilton one afternoon along with my usual crew of misfits, when we came across an intriguing poster.

The poster featured a drawing of a completely naked woman along with knives, skulls and other representations of nasty heavy metal. "The Sinisters" was scrolled across the top in bold letters followed by "Live at the Corktown" as well as the date of the show.

The fact that we were all under-age didn't faze us a bit and we became determined not to miss this supposed spectacle of sin.

The night of the big show arrived. Brenda and I had the guys over at Amityville after school and we started drinking early.

When you're underage and/or poor, it's always a good idea to be drunk before entering the bar, that way you can avoid having to approach the bar staff once you get inside.

That is, if you can even get inside. Brenda and I were dressed in our most provocative black rags.

For some reason, teenage girls always seem to think that dressing slutty will make them appear older. It's a common misconception. The only way this improves your situation is if: a) the doorman is a pig or b) you're looking to get laid. Anyway, we emerged from the apartment sufficiently wasted and eagerly staggered over to the Corktown.

The best way to avoid an ugly confrontation with an obnoxious door person is to show up before they've permanently planted their ass at the entrance.

Simply slide in quietly and confine yourself to the washroom (bring along a beer, you'll be there a while).

Then after the club begins to fill with people and the band starts, just casually join the crowd gathered in front of the stage. This method is practically failsafe. Practically.

That night the plan was working well, at first.

I had managed to rendezvous with the others and we were in the process of congratulating ourselves when I saw him. He was the wildest, most unapologetic punk rocker I'd ever seen. His name was Steve Saint. I watched in awe as he violently spat out the words that accompanied the onslaught of angry noise.

Wearing a pair of hot pink and black stripped stockings, and a pair of shiny red high heels, he contorted and madly flung himself around the stage.

His short black hair was spiked erratically and his eyes were smeared with dark eyeliner.

"He's perfect!" I yelled to Brenda and she nodded her head laughing.

Suddenly, I felt someone grab hold of my arm and I was spun around only to find myself face to face with the biggest, ugliest, white trash woman in the world.

"Where's your ID?" She croaked.

"Get your fuckin' hands off me," I snapped back tearing my arm from her grip.

Brenda and the rest of my company did their best to back step into the shadows but it was too late, the horrible ogre woman had spotted them.

There's nothing quite as amusing as watching an overweight klutz trying to chase and capture a handful of obnoxious, inebriated teenagers. She never stood a chance.

The audience cheered us on as we leapt over chairs and raced around the pool tables each taunting her in turn. Of course, the harder everyone laughed, the angrier the she-ogre got. Saint screamed a few choice words over the microphone in her direction and that was it. She called the cops and we split before they showed up.

In a unanimous decision to reject defeat and all its consequences, we congregated behind the club.

It was time for plan B.

We walked the short distance back to Amityville and had another drink.

Then I ransacked the closet for some disguises. All I could find was a couple of toques, a feather boa, a black scarf, a pink wig and some army fatigues.

It was the middle of the summer but once we were re-dressed, we looked like we were ready for a snow storm.

Satisfied, we gathered our collective courage and started back towards the Corktown.

Just before we reached the club, we split up in hopes of improving our odds of re-entrance.

I led Brenda to the back door while the guys chose to try the front. Just as I'd hoped, the loading door was left unlocked.

We silently slipped in beside the stage to see the last of their set.

Brian Sinister (the drummer) spotted us despite our flimsy attempt to appear inconspicuous, and laughing, pointed us out to the rest of the band.

He then motioned to our cohorts who had also made it back into the bar.

Our disguises were ridiculous. The guys looked like they were on their way to rob a bank.

"Welcome back," Saint stupidly shouted into the microphone and sure enough, we turned around just in time to see the huge red faced she-ogre striding towards us.

This time however, she knew the full-on fiasco that awaited her and was returning with re-enforcements.

We were escorted out of the bar for the second time that evening by two police officers who then told us to go home. Back at the apartment we all agreed that it was well worth it. The Sinisters left a lasting impression on me and they would not soon forget the crazy little seventeen-year-old that went through so much trouble just to see one of their shows.

Not long after that I began promoting shows in Hamilton and brought them back to play a few times.

When I turned twenty, they asked me to be on their album cover.

The record was called Cheerleader Drug Dealer.

Little did I know that in only a couple of years I would have the pleasure of playing with both Brian and Saint.

With their help (and the support of so many others), I released my first album "Rock Action" in the spring of 2001.

"The Sinisters" never made it big, but their shows were legendary, their integrity was flawless, and their spirit unstoppable.

11
Eating Ashes
Craig and the crack house

My second apartment was a small, split level semi-detached located in the low rent district of Hamilton's east end.

The day after I moved in, I baked some chocolate chip cookies in hopes of winning over my new neighbours.

I had a feeling that I would be giving them plenty of reasons to complain in the near future.

I knocked on the first door and heard the dogs on the other side barking ferociously.

The door then creaked opened a crack and a bloodshot eye stared menacingly at me through the gap. A second later it swung wide open and two huge Dobermans came charging out at me. They looked and acted as if they hadn't been fed in weeks. I was terrified but stood my ground. Just before they reached me, they were jolted backwards by their steel collars (the kind with the spikes on the inside).

There in the dark doorway stood a thick skinned old hag.

She glared at me suspiciously and I uncomfortably introduced myself. To my surprise, the wrinkled witch invited me in (although hesitantly) and quickly confined her hell hounds to the bedroom. Her dishevelled apartment reeked of urine and stale cigarette smoke. It was painfully clear that she lived alone, was on the dole and was way too paranoid to leave the house on any regular basis.

She thanked me for the cookies and offered me a scotch.

She must have been desperate for the company because within ten minutes, she had told me her entire life story.

Apparently her ex-husband was an abusive alcoholic convict who had sworn to kill her and now she was in hiding. I knew she was serious when she reached under the couch and pulled out a fully loaded, sawed off shotgun.

Unnerved, I swallowed my scotch and made a polite exit. At least I knew she wouldn't be a rat or anything, and I'd take sharing space with a psycho over a square any day.

I had only been living there for about a month, when I got a call from an old friend who needed a place to stay.

Craig was a career criminal that I had met while living downtown. He was tough, dangerous and totally hilarious.

Craig was calling from the Barton St. jail where he'd just been released. I had always had a great time with him, so I told him he could crash at my place for a day or two.

By the end of the week he had swept me off my feet and we had become an item. After that, he wasted no time in filling the apartment with stolen goods. Each night I'd come home from work to find cameras and stereos stashed throughout the flat. One time I walked in and he had stolen a six foot long, black leather bar with a white marble counter top. I must confess, at first it was kind of exciting and even romantic in a demented way.

However, any attraction I'd felt towards Craig was obliterated when he got hooked on crack. Within a few weeks I was coming home to an apartment infested with disgusting middle-age scum bags. They were mostly dealers, crack whores and petty thieves, except for one-legged Kim.

Kim had been in a horrible car crash. She'd lost her leg and was awarded a huge cash settlement. She was the nicest of the bunch. In exchange for tolerating her constant presence, she granted me unlimited use of her brand new Mercedes. I drove it everywhere, (despite the fact that I didn't have a license) teaching myself how in the process.

Between working at the Ritz and traveling, I was hardly ever there. The worse it got at home, the more I found ways of staying away. I always felt sorry for the scrawny, bruised up hookers that would stop by to score. A couple of them were about my age and I'd cook them a meal whenever I had the time. When I stopped paying rent to prompt an eviction, the landlord came to the house and the dealers actually covered it for me.

By then, the place had become a total heat-score and my sharp intuition told me it was time to leave. I sold the six foot boa constrictor that my father had gotten me for my fifteenth birthday to a traveling stripper that I had met at the club. I packed a few bags (as much stuff as I could carry), and left the majority of my belongings behind.

Before I left, I dropped a signed letter of abandonment in the landlord's post box. I was so pissed off that I never told Craig that I was leaving, nor did I say good-bye. Spunky Megs had offered to let me crash with her for a while, and, after living with Craig, I was glad to have the opportunity to share a space with a girl again.

The following week I returned to the house with the intention of salvaging some more of my stuff. My section of the small apartment complex had been sealed of with yellow police tape. The place had been raided and everyone there had been thrown in jail. Everything that had once filled my home had been ransacked and heaped into a pile on the cement lawn. All my possessions had been destroyed. There was nothing I could do except take a deep breath, keep on walking and not look back.

12
Club Ritz

After stripping illegally for a few months in St. Catherines I got tired of the two hour daily commute back and forth. More specifically, I was sick of the annoying chicks in my car pool.

I decided to drop my so called "manager" and search for a club that would be closer to home. The first bar I went to was "Club Ritz."

I was still somewhat naïve about the adult entertainment business and eager to start making money. Anxiously, I accepted their strict rules and regulations unaware of the freedom that would be offered at other local bars.

At "the Ritz," the night shift started at four o'clock in the afternoon and went straight on 'till two am. During that time no girls were allowed to leave the bar (not even the freelancers) and there were no breaks.

Drugs were strictly prohibited and any and all girls that were caught drunk on the job were promptly sent home.

The tiny club was usually empty and the shift pay was under minimum wage. The management ran the place like Nazis, keeping us all repressed under their anal regime. It was only due to the friends that I made while working there that I stayed for an entire year.

On my first night I was approached by a sweet and petite blonde girl named Spunky Megs. She told me that I reminded her of a friend that she had back in high school named Brenda. It turned out to be the very same Brenda whom I had lived with the previous year, and whose ID I was still borrowing to dance with. It was incredible how much Spunky and I had in common and within a few days of hanging out together, we were inseparable. I left my criminally insane crack-head boyfriend and moved in to her tiny bachelor apartment.

One afternoon we were working at the bar when I spotted a freaky looking bald guy walk in wearing pink prescription glasses and a "Primus" t-shirt (one of my favourite bands at the time). He wasn't the slightest bit sexy, but since I had nothing better to do I went over and introduced myself.

I figured at the very least I could kill some time talking about music (my favourite conversational topic). He told me his name was Shane and that he drove a transport truck.

He had a great sense of humour and an obsession for drugs and rock n' roll that almost equalled mine. We spent the entire evening laughing and getting wasted and although I never danced for him, he still gave me a couple hundred dollars for my time.

Over the next few months Shane came back to the club to visit us whenever he was in town and before long Spunky and I were hanging out with him outside of work.

He always treated us with total respect and never once came on to either of us. After a while Shane became like a big brother, so when he asked me to join him on his next trip to L.A. (all expenses paid plus some spending cash), I jumped at the opportunity.

Once on the road with Shane I realized what a huge speed freak he was. He'd stay awake for days popping over-the-counter speed pills and snorting something called "crank." Crank was the most abrasive substance I've ever abused. In a futile attempt to take the edge off, I bought a huge bottle of whiskey, which we shared as we sped south. Doing rails felt like snorting a combination of glass and fire. The high was comparable to being on coke, crystal meth and acid all at the same time. Shane was so wasted that I even convinced him to let me drive for a while. Some of the happiest times of my life have been while on the road to nowhere.

By the time we reached Arizona I was completely peaking and was amazed at Shane's ability to stay on the road. It seemed my vision was always the first to go and by then, it was clear that my eyes could no longer be trusted.

As the sun set across the desert, I stared out the window and the horizon became an electric liquid. I sat in awe as the vibrant waves of warmth came cascading towards me, consuming me. After dark I saw ghostly apparitions of huge white horses galloping steadily in front of the rig.

During the next night, a brilliant storm broke out high above us. It was an incredible display of nature's power. Pale blue lightening slashed through the dark clouds horizontally as we raced towards the blazing sky with the stereo on high. That week had been so intense that I was actually relieved when we ran out of crank. That is, until we reached Barstow, California, a few hours later and Shane bought another two-week supply.

Before reaching L.A., we stopped in Vegas for a few days because Shane's sister was getting married. The ceremony took place at "The Little White Chapel" which (famous or not) was one of the cheapest and tackiest places I've ever seen. I couldn't understand why the happy couple (and both sets of parents) had flown all the way down from Alberta just to be married in a white-washed shack. It was pretty sad.

Shane and I went gambling in the casinos and I actually started to win some cash. That is of course, until they kicked me out for being under-age and took it all back. Bastards! I'd bet that if I had been losing money, they would have let me sit there all night.

I think it's so stupid that Americans can't drink alcohol until they're twenty-one. Consider the facts, at sixteen any half-competent kid can go get their license and drive a car or truck. They can legally control a big metal machine that moves really fast and has the potential to kill a number of people including the driver. Booze on the other hand (at its worst), has the unnerving capability to make one act foolish, throw up, and wake up feeling really bad the next day. Which one of these tasks do you think would require the greater level of maturity?

For me, Southern California was love at first sight. I was jealous of every little house that was cradled between the lush hills and cursed the night that I was born in Canada.

I had the chance to swim in the second of both oceans and swore that I would return someday soon. I took full advantage of the long drive home to catch up on some sleep and attempted to level myself out. My waking hours were spent writing and sharing personal stories with Shane.

While I was trying to clear my head by briefly refraining from hard drugs, Shane was parting just as hard as he had during the drive down. I was amazed at his chemical tolerance. His lifestyle was completely psychotic and yet he still managed to function sufficiently. What I mean is, he never put us in a ditch or anything like that. Above all else, Shane taught me to always get the job done, regardless of how stoned you are at the time. There are no worthy excuses and no such thing as "too chewed to move."

Over the next few years I took any opportunity that I had to travel with Shane and by doing so I was able to see most of North America before my twentieth birthday.

One night while we were in Ft. Lauderdale, we found a party on the beach and met some cool locals. After downing a few beers, I thought it would be fun to jump into the ocean along with a couple of surfer guys that I was hanging out with. I was wet up to my waist when a huge wave sent me tumbling over. When I stood back up the Americans were staring at me wide eyed and utterly confused. Within moments I realized why. In my drunken enthusiasm I had forgotten that I had been wearing my long blonde wig that night, and as a result the powerful wave had swiftly ripped it off my head and claimed it for its own.

There I stood with my conspicuously shaved head shining in the moonlight. It freaked the guys out so bad; they bolted for the shore like I was a shark. It was classic.

The only trip with Shane that ended badly was one we took to Atlanta to watch "the Winston Cup" NASCAR races. The day after the big event we had to unrepentantly pick up this disgusting fat couple from Shane's trucking company. They had killed some people in a head-on highway collision the night before, and to Shane and me they seemed arrogantly unremorseful. It was brutal! We were suddenly expected to give them a lift home, which to us meant the party was over. This couple truly was the literal definition of trailer trash. I lasted about an hour in the company of such extreme ignorance before I totally lost it.

I asked Shane for everything in his wallet (which amounted to just over a hundred dollars and threw some clothes and make-up into a plastic grocery bag. Shane promised to return the rest of my luggage later and dropped me off at a bus stop downtown. Luckily, I had exactly enough cash for a ticket to Toronto, not a dollar more. I rode back on the greyhound bus alone and for three days I neither ate nor drank. I met human greed, selfishness and disregard straight in the face and there was no sympathy.

Once back in Toronto, I met up with some friends and went directly to a "Cramps" concert. As much as I loved traveling, it always felt good to be back on my own turf.

As for Club Ritz, one night Spunky Megs and I were caught smoking a joint in the change room closet and after exchanging some choice words with the management, I was fired without pay. I've always felt that everything in life (including the negative) happens for a reason and although it didn't seem like a good thing at the time, it ultimately pushed me towards bigger and better things.

13
69 Paradise

I was eighteen when Marc called me looking for a roommate. His father had just bought a house in Westdale and if Marc was able to fill it with his friends, then he would be allowed to live there for free as the superintendent.

The house had two stories and two separate apartments. The downstairs unit had four bedrooms while the upstairs apartment only had two. I jumped at the opportunity to live in yet another party house and signed on to take one of the cheaper rooms downstairs. It was going to be me and five guys. Even the address was wild; 69 Paradise Rd.

As soon as we moved in we converted the basement into a bare bones rehearsal space and practiced there until the neighbours complained so much that we started getting fined by the police. Damn cops. About a block away there was an amazing public pool that was surrounded by a ten foot high chain link fence. It would have taken a hell of a lot more than that to keep us out though. After dark, the pool became our own private playground and there were plenty of midnight skinny dipping sessions.

The great thing about living there was that all my roommates were all just as crazy as me. We weren't afraid of being shunned by society for our excessive and unusual lifestyles. 69 Paradise was a house free of inhibitions.

We created a place that was beyond rules and responsibility. Most of the tenants were musicians and those that weren't were hard core fans of live music. At the time there wasn't exactly much of a music scene in Hamilton, so we built our own. I started promoting rock shows at the Corktown and at another local venue called Grapes n' Things. Most of the shows involved friends of mine, such as Riotstar, The High School Hookers and The Sinisters. It seems like I've always had to find ways of making my own fun.

The Riotstar house was always open to our friends and there was never a monotonous moment.

Every night was an entirely new party and there was a constant supply of drugs and alcohol. We took whatever we could get our hands on, from mescaline to morphine, but our steady diet consisted mainly of freebase and heroin.

The front lawn was littered with broken beer bottles, used needles, empty crack cans and many more items that belonged in a biohazard bag.

One day, a friend stopped by and gave me a bottle of expired liquid Demerol. I had no previous experience with Demerol and wasn't quite sure what to do with it.

I assumed that it would be a similar buzz to the opiates that we had been using, and so I called Marc into my room and filled a syringe. Back then, he and I were partners in crime. I've always made the same deal with my boyfriends. They were allowed to do whatever drugs they wanted, as long as they shared them with me, and vice versa.

This time it was Marc who volunteered to try the first shot. I tied him off and injected the clear liquid straight into his vein. He stood up, took about three steps and then fell face first onto the hallway floor. He didn't even raise his hands to break his fall and he hit the floor with a loud THUD.

Right away I knew something had gone terribly wrong. I called out to our roommates in a panic, telling them to call 911. They flooded into the hall just in time to see him start to convulse and foam at the mouth. Smashing his face on the cheap linoleum had left him with a bloody nose, a gash in his forehead and two black eyes.

We rolled him over and blood began to gush from his wounds. This was the first major overdose I'd seen, but what really made me nervous was that it was entirely my fault. I stood there dumbfounded wondering whether or not I had just killed my boyfriend.

While I wasn't afraid to die young, I didn't want to be the reason someone else died (at least not someone I loved).

By the time the ambulance showed up, Marc had regained consciousness, although he was still delirious and making absolutely no sense. I told the paramedics what happened and they explained to me that unlike morphine, Demerol was not a mainline drug. It was supposed to be injected into a large muscle, not a vein.

I felt like such an idiot. Marc later told me that in those few brief moments, he had literally seen his life flash before his eyes. I knew then that if he did die that day, at least he would do so knowing that he had lived his life to the fullest.

Living at 69 Paradise was like living in a modern commune. The six of us became so close, so fast, and were always so screwed up, that in no time we had formed our own little Manson family. Living in such an unstructured situation and being completely removed from the rest of the world makes it easy to lose touch with reality. Or at least what the general population considers to be reality.

For us, those days were all about freedom, hard drugs and rock n' roll. I stayed at the Riotstar house for over two years. I consider those times to be among the best of my life and whenever I remember them, I still wish that I could go back and do it all again.

I wouldn't change a thing.

14
Punkfest

Punkfest was an all ages/all welcome party that took place in the small northern Ontario town of Marmora. I first heard about the event from Marc, who had attended the previous season. He raved about it and told me that he had done so much PCP, he thought he was going to die.

This sounded too wild for me to pass up, so when July of '97 rolled around, we packed up our coke dealers van and set out on the four hour drive.

We knew there was going to be an entry fee of fifteen dollars per person. So shortly before we reached the main gate we stopped so some of us could hop the fence.

We darted into the dark bushes and easily scaled the rusty wire. I had other plans for my cash.

Once inside, I couldn't believe my eyes. I was in punk rock paradise. People from all over the world had come to camp out, get wasted and listen to the music that we all loved. These were people that I knew I could relate to, kids that really lived the scene.

The official name of the grounds was Spiderland in honour of the creepy old hermit that owned the place. The vast property stretched out over acres of untamed wilderness and was divided down the middle by a narrow winding path affectionately called Anarchy Alley.

My first order of business was to track down some of this PCP I'd heard so much about. As I strolled down the alley I noticed that most of the campsites had home-made cardboard signs listing the variety of drugs they had available for sale. These illegible posters were tied or nailed to the nearby trees. It didn't take long for me to find one advertising exactly what I was looking for. This particular camp belonged to a bunch of street kids from

Montreal. They explained to me as best they could in a mix of broken English and muddy Quebecois, that the drugs were not only dirt cheap (by my standards), but readily available where they were from. I decided they all looked and sounded sufficiently messed up, so I bought five small baggies of shimmering white powder for fifty bucks. Satisfied, I thanked them and started back to my friends.

Along the way I was pleasantly surprised to see hundreds of die-hard fanatics getting along so harmoniously. During my stay, I never witnessed one confrontation (verbal or otherwise) and no one's property was damaged or stolen. That weekend we were all united against the world. Together we were safe and strong.

Finally, I found the van parked near the front gate. By then the guys had managed to build a healthy fire and those fortunate enough to have supplies were organizing them. I grabbed Marc's arm and motioned to our roommates to follow. We huddled under a nearby tree and lit a book of matches so I could see what I was doing. I cut up a round of fat lines on an old Iggy Pop CD and snorted a generous heap. Immediately my face began to burn and my eyes filled with tears. For a moment I thought my nose was bleeding.

"Holy Shit," I said as I passed the CD. When everyone had done some, we looked at each other grinning ear to ear with wide, bloodshot eyes. The poison quickly started to saturate our soft flesh and drip down the backs of our throats. Suddenly we were invincible! Not only could I no longer feel my body, but the world around me became warped in a wonderful new way. It was unlike any other buzz that I had experienced before. I picked up a stone and turned it over in my hand, fascinated with its cool smoothness. I felt as light and free as a feather in the wind.

Before long, all basic bodily functions such as eating, drinking and sleeping became obsolete. After a steady pace of substance abuse nothing mattered but being together.

We pooled our cash and invested in more of our new favourite drug. I hid our stash (enough to keep us all glowing for the next month) in the van and went to watch the bands that were playing on the main stage.

The weekend was loud, dirty and crowded. Bands were playing 'round the clock on three separate stages. The music surrounded us and we appreciated the chaotic, abrasive sound. It kept me awake the entire time.

We also went skinny dipping in a nearby river and dried ourselves on the warm grass. Punkfest ended as abruptly as it began when, without warning our driver announced it was time to go home. One by one we obediently filed into the vehicle and I pushed my way to the front.

"Can't we just keep driving south?" I asked full of hope. My only reply was a chuckle from our driver who unlike the rest of us, had not indulged in any PCP. He just couldn't relate. At least we were all headed back to our party house, not much chance of reality's ugly claws sinking in there.

My roommates and I remained on our strict new diet of drugs until one morning I could no longer see my own outstretched hand. My vision had become limited to about one foot in front of my face and my eyes couldn't stop crossing. I started to worry they might be permanently damaged and decided the best remedy was to drink my face off. Hard liquor always seems to flush out my system.

That night we hosted an all-out house party and polished off what was left of the chemical. Two days later, I woke up on my filthy bedroom floor with my vision restored. At the time, I was so poor that I still didn't have a mattress or dresser. I looked around at my pitiful belongings piled around me in heaps of disarray. I felt so free. I was surrounded by friends and had absolutely nothing to lose. Punkfest showed me sometimes poverty can be a luxury.

15
High School Hookers

I'll never forget the night I met Jelly James. He was a local musician infamous for his outrageous antics as a lead singer. Jelly was the founding member of a group called "The High School Hookers." If there was anyone in the area who could pull off Glam Rock in full drag, it was Jelly James.

He had recently returned to Hamilton to live with his long-time girlfriend Sue, after staying for a stretch in Toronto at the Elmocambo and partying non-stop with promoter Dan Burke.

"Riotstar" was scheduled to play some second-rate battle of the bands which was being held at the Ramada Hotel in downtown Hamilton, but they were short a bass player.

Jelly had graciously agreed to fill in for the gig.

The minute we walked into the gutted out conference room, all heads turned towards us.

We appeared shockingly out of place surrounded by uninspiring post-grunge influenced bands. While every other kid in the room was dressed to work a shift at the nearest gas station, we strutted in decked out in rubber, tight black leather, fun fur coats and glitter make-up.

We took one glance around the room, then turned on our heels and headed straight for the women's washroom. It was time for refreshments.

Seconds later the bathroom door swung open and two cops came bursting in, sealing the only exit behind them. The lame-ass gig was so uptight, that they had hired pigs to chaperone the non-event.

Fuckin' traitors! It felt like we had been set up. After all, if they wanted a pop and chip party they should have known better than to invite a notorious group of rowdies like us.

We were then harshly ordered to empty the contents of our pockets (my purse included) and place any and all objects on the counter by the sink. It has generally been my experience that by politely complying with a police officer's request, most of the time, they'll let you off a little easier. It's the liars that they really hate. Reluctantly, we pulled out our private possessions which of course, consisted of a variety of drug paraphernalia (rolling papers, glass pipes, flasks of hard liquor, syringes, burnt spoons, etc.), as well an assortment of small weapons. My illegal switch blade was immediately confiscated. Damn Cops.

It was only due to Jelly's smooth talking and my stealthy ability to conceal a stash at the speed of light, that we narrowly evaded being arrested right there. This was obviously not the first time Jelly had given this speech and together we made a great team. However, as a result of our confrontation, the band was immediately disqualified from the competition and we were escorted directly out of the hotel. We had only been there a total of ten minutes.

Back out on the street I sarcastically suggested that maybe the other bands had sized us up and fearfully sabotaged our spot. After all, we were the professionals, not to mention the best dressed gang in town.

Those kids had merely deprived themselves of an opportunity to witness the real deal up close and personal.

Disappointed in the unfortunate turn of events, half the band took off to the bar while Marc, Jelly and I headed for a "safe use" house he knew of that was nearby.

The house was run by a guy in his late twenties with long blonde dreadlocks named Frank. Marc and I had barely begun our introductions when Jelly collapsed onto the floor with a needle still hanging limply out of his arm.

He thrashed around for a moment convulsing and then became very still. Concerned, I asked Frank if we should call an ambulance or something.

"Oh, don't worry about him," he replied, "He does this all the time. Why do you think we call him Jelly?"

This was by no means my first experience with overdose, but that didn't make the situation any less shocking.

"Stay here with him a minute and I'll be right back," Frank sighed, sensing his words offered me little comfort.

Within minutes he returned with an ice cream bar which he then force fed to our new friend. For some strange reason, it worked almost as well as a shot of adrenaline because moments later Jelly was sitting up and we had resumed our conversation like nothing had happened. From that moment on, I never stressed out about Jelly again.

After that, "The High School Hookers" became regular guests at the Riotstar house. We'd sit around listening to records, exchanging crazy stories and getting high.

It was at one of these casual get-togethers that Jelly extended to me an invitation to become an honorary member of his band. Although I was way too stoned to sing that night, I gladly accepted his offer.

We started rehearsals the next day. Sue and I sang back-ups together and became good friends. Before long, we had a weekly gig playing every Tuesday night at a small bar in Hess Village. We never made any money and half the time the band was nodding out mid-song, but despite ourselves we still managed to acquire a small cult following.

Singing with "The Hookers" gave me the confidence and experience I needed to dive back into my own music. I always had a great time performing with them, but could never truly be satisfied having to share the spot light.

16
Close Call

Among the riskiest endeavours that I've participated in, was a "business" trip to the Caribbean Islands.

At the time I was nineteen and living with Marc at the Riotstar house. It was there, at one of our weekend bashes that one of my dealers casually pulled me aside.

"I have a proposition for you" he said under his breath.

I had known John for over a year. He was a fixture at Club Ritz and I had met him while I was working there. He sold crystal meth, coke and E to the dancers and he was relatively reliable.

Like most pushers he was physically repulsive, towering at six and a half feet and weighing over three hundred pounds. John would often stop by the house unannounced knowing that he was guaranteed make a few sales.

I kicked a crowd of drunken friends out of my bedroom and we sat down on the bed. John cut up some rails on a CD case.

"OK, let's hear it," I said.

"Ever been to the Caribbean?" he asked and paused to snort a small pile of cocaine before passing the disc to me.

"If you want the job," he continued, "You'll be one of five people, including myself, who are going to the islands for a couple of weeks. It's all expenses paid and when we get back I'll give you a thousand dollars cash. That's the easy part."

He paused, put out two more lines and this time offered the disc to me before doing one. "The hard part?" He lowered his voice: "We're bringing back fifty kilos of uncut coke."

"And how exactly?" I asked grinning.

"It's simple" he said with a coy smile. "Each couple will have two separate return tickets. One directly to Toronto, the other with a stop-over in Miami. We check in the bag, you know the bag preparing to board the express flight, then flush the ticket and board the plane to Florida. By the time they figure out what's happened, which I doubt they will, we'll be safely out of the country with nothing illegal tracing back to us." We sat in silence for a moment while I contemplated the plan. It just might work, I thought to myself. As an avid drug user and abuser I felt it was a worthy cause and besides, I really needed the money.

"OK," I said with hidden reluctance. "I'm in."

While we were all departing at the same time, we were not coming back together. The plan was for the first fake couple to leave the islands after ten days with thirty kilos.

John and the other two were going to follow after thirteen days with the remaining twenty.

Being superstitious, I knew better than to sign up for the latter. Unfortunately the other girl had the same idea.

Luckily for me, greed got the best of her. She demanded to be paid the thousand dollars up front before she would agree to go anywhere.

John reluctantly paid her on the condition that she take the second flight home and stop being such a bitch. That was just fine by me. After all, I was used to being poor.

The next day I had my passport photo redone in an attempt to look more respectable. Still, covering my tattoos and removing my piercings could not subdue my rebellious style so I went savaging for preppy clothes at the Salvation

Army. Before I knew it, it was time to leave and the stretch limo slowly pulled up in front of the house. Marc wrapped his arms around me in silent protest. Our eyes met and without a word, we said good-bye.

Inside the limo I was greeted by the rest of the group.

John was there, as well as two other occupants that I recognized from the Ritz. Shelly, who was a "house girl," which meant she'd spent the worst part of a decade stripping at the same bar.

Shelly had long crispy hair that had been bleached, permed and teased too often and she wore her bangs in the classic 80's mall-claw. Single and desperately clinging to her thirties, it was clear why she was making the trip.

Sitting to her left was Ben who ran the snack bar at the Ritz. Need I say more? The final passenger was introduced to me as Nick, a friend of Ben's and equally unimpressive.

"Wow, what a crew" I said although nobody caught my sarcasm. It already looked like I'd be earning every penny.

It was going to be my first plane ride and I was expecting to love it. I'd spent so many psychedelic trips gazing at the clouds and straining to touch the sky. My time to soar had arrived. We boarded the plane and my hopes were dashed when I was seated not at a window, but in the aisle. I strapped myself in and soon we were in the air.

Suddenly it felt as if someone had sunk a screwdriver into each of my ears. My eyes watered and I clapped my hands over my ears anticipating a warm stream of blood to come gushing out of each orifice.

When I looked at my hands however, they were dry. A few hours later the sharp pain had receded into a throbbing ache that was accompanied by a high pitch ringing. It took almost two days for the headache to finally surrender.

It was then (like a typical Leo), I decided that my feet belonged firmly on the ground.

Once we arrived in St. Lucia we rented a topless jeep and drove out to the hotel. The small island was breathtaking.

Up until then, it was the closest I'd come to actual paradise. Shelly and I shared a double room and the guys stayed in a room across the pool.

The first day we were there we went to the local marketplace. All the money I had in the world was a Canadian twenty dollar bill tucked inside my passport (in case of an extreme emergency), so while the others shopped for souvenirs I went out in search of some tropical wild flowers to press and dry in my notebook.

Ignorant of the Caribbean heat, I had purchased my second-hand travel wardrobe with the sole intention of concealing my tattoos. I was wearing blue jeans, a long sleeve white blouse and combat boots (the only footwear I owned at the time). The island sun had me down within ten minutes.

I don't remember fainting but I woke up surrounded by panicking native women trying to drown me.

They were yelling in an unfamiliar language and dousing me with bottles of the most potent rum in existence. I tried to open my eyes to get a grasp of what was happening but the alcohol burned like acid.

I gasped for air and managed to scramble away a few feet before I realized that I was covered on my own vomit.

My accomplices soon saw the commotion and came over to retrieve me, thanking the women for their help. That was the day I discovered heat stroke.

I spent the following three days confined to my quarters recovering.

When I eventually started feeling a bit better I joined the gang in visiting a volcano.

Brian had found a weed connection the previous evening so we spent the morning smoking and drinking pina coladas. As if our liquid breakfast combined with the long winding mountain road wasn't enough to resurrect my nausea, the rotten egg smell of the volcano pushed me right back over the edge. Once again I was sick on myself while the others took pictures posing as tourists.

Before we left I suggested that we smoke a few more joints, as weed sometimes settles my stomach. It made no difference though. The stench of sulphur was too severe.

Then as if the sky had swayed to show me some mercy, it began to rain.

We quickly piled back into the jeep with false expectations of shelter. John sunk the gas pedal to the floor and we raced down the mountain.

The dirt road was so narrow that two cars couldn't pass each other. As we slid through the unpredictable hills at top speed I gazed out at the wet jungle and began to get stressed.

All it would have taken was another vehicle or even a stray dog to send us plunging over the side. I could just imagine a rolled jeep and our crew half dead and hidden in the thick vegetation of the rainforest. No one would be searching for us and no emergency paramedics would be dispatched to the scene. At every corner I braced myself for it. I spent the entire thirty minute stretch back to civilization poised in crash position with my eyes shut tight. That's the only negative side affect of marijuana, the occasional paranoia.

The next day, it was back on a plane as we flew to St. Martin. To my pleasant surprise this island was much more modern and tourist friendly.

We stayed at a hotel that was on the beach right beside a beautiful resort. In a last desperate attempt to have some fun I joined Ben, who had rented a jet ski for the afternoon.

The ocean was clear and warm. He even let me drive for a little while. I've never been a fan of water sports because of the swimming factor, but jet skiing was different. It was the best time I had on the whole trip.

We spent the remaining few days lounging around at the hotel and basking in the sun. I had my blonde hair braided and beaded and worked on a tan to try to fit in with the normal vacationers.

At last it was time to leave. I couldn't wait to send the drugs because it meant I was going home. Such relief may have had a hand in helping me through customs on that hot Caribbean night. It also didn't hurt that we weren't the only ones sweating.

We were careful to use a different agent each time we checked our luggage. I flushed our decoy tickets down the toilets in the modest airport restroom and met Ben outside for a cigarette. A simple wink let him know it was done.

I wasn't able to really relax until I was half-way home and we had landed in Miami. We were only scheduled for a two hour stop-over, no a big deal, but then (of course) the flight was delayed additional eight.

With ten anxious hours to kill and no cash, I made some collect calls, drank lots of water and unsuccessfully attempted to sleep on the floor. By the time we landed back in Toronto I was so sick of my pretend partner (Ben) that I was coming very close to strangling him at any moment. I couldn't wait to get out of there.

Once in the terminal at Pearson, we were pulled into Canadian customs. After our bags were ripped apart, we were strip-searched and interrogated, but with no evidence they were forced to release us both. To top it off, our driver failed to show up and was not responding to his pager. I couldn't stand it anymore!

I picked up my belongings and headed towards the freeway on foot. I was no stranger to hitch-hiking so I hit the nearest on-ramp and stuck out my thumb. It wasn't until I was picked up that I realized I was going the wrong way.

In a panic I asked to be dropped off at the nearest downtown exit.

From there I dragged my luggage for forty-five minutes (cursing the day I'd ever heard of the Caribbean), while walking to Union Station. Pulling out my passport and my precious twenty dollar bill, I bought a one-way train ticket back to Hamilton. My ordeal was finally over.

Back at the house, my real boyfriend and I locked ourselves our room for three days. The only thing that lured me out was a visit from John and Ben. Fantastic, I thought. Time to get paid! Soon it would all be worth it. I cleared the common room and the two of them sat down across from me on the couch.

"I've got some bad news," John said looking at the floor. "Shelly and Nick never made it back. They were busted on the Island before they even boarded the plane. Caught with twenty kilos. Their families have hired lawyers."

For a long moment no one spoke.

"Where's my money?" I demanded sternly, staring him straight in the eyes.

"As I've said, there have been some complications," he replied shifting uncomfortably in his seat. "I'll have it for you as soon as everything gets sorted out."

I showed them the door and never heard from them again.

So, in the end I didn't get my money, but I didn't get a prison sentence either.

I looked back at my pressed purple flowers with a whole new appreciation. I knew that I had gotten the best souvenir of all.

17
Hanrahan's

After I was fired from the extremely anal Club Ritz for smoking weed, I once again resumed my search for a normal, respectable job. Unfortunately, without a high school diploma, previous experience or any credible references the task seemed daunting to say the least.

After a few weeks of rejection, I reluctantly bit the bullet and started dancing at a club called Hanrahan's. The bar was located in Hamilton's north end, directly across the road from the Barton Street Jail and surrounded by half-way houses. Of all the strip clubs in the city Hanrahan's had the worst reputation.

It was not unusual to witness one or more bar fights a week there. The cops were a permanent presence, but spent the majority of their time watching the stage and flirting with the girls. In essence, they were completely useless. It didn't take long for me to make myself at home. And all the excitement was a welcome change from the boredom of some of the other strip clubs I'd worked.

By discreetly asking a few questions to the right people I easily learned where to go for all my drug needs. The manager sold mushrooms and hash on occasion, the enormous bouncer sold crack in forty dollar pieces, the DJ could score almost any kind of pill on request and a couple of the house girls provided powder cocaine and/or heroin for the right price. Substance abuse was so openly accepted and rampant that an average wait for a washroom stall in the ladies room was between five and ten minutes. I fit right in, which for me, was a first.

Drug fiends make fast friends. Mostly because very few people are willing to deal with them and they're often terribly lonely at times. Therefore when someone is nice to them, they remember. Even the junkies working at Hanrahan's were generous and there was always more than enough stuff to go around. In short, business was good. I managed to buy my first car, rent a nice rehearsal studio downtown and order my first batch of band shirts.

I had half the girls in the bar wearing black "CJ Sleez and the S.T.D's" under-shirts while hustling at the bar. I couldn't have asked for better advertising.

It was during these two years that I wrote the majority of my first album including the song "Gutter Dolls." This song was based on two girls that I knew from the club. One of them was found dead by her four-year-old fatherless son.

She had been main-lining crack, which is down-right insane in my educated opinion. The part about the little boy made it tragic. Her best friend took the week off work and now that she was home in the evenings spending time with her husband, she became suspicious of his odd outings and strange sketched-out behaviour. She had never noticed it before, or so she said when she called me crying. She was convinced he was cheating on her. I suggested she chill out and search for some proof. That was the last we ever spoke.

I read about what happened in the newspaper a few days later. After doing a bit of light detective work around her house she found a grocery bag hidden behind the furnace. It was stuffed with a selection of blood stained women's under garments. Frantically, she continued to tear the house apart but was unable find anything else incriminating.

That's when she decided to go through the garbage bags that had been piled precariously at the end of her driveway by her husband, days before their scheduled pick-up.

What she found in those bags changed her life forever.

Neatly packed and wrapped in plastic were the dismembered body parts of several young women.

Another shady character that I met at Hanrahan's was a dealer named Dave. He would host after-hours parties at his place for the girls and the few boyfriends that he considered trustworthy. Whenever we went over there, Marc would earn a little extra cash by breaking up huge bricks of hash into quarter ounce squares. Although Marc couldn't hold a real job, I always found ways to make him useful and Dave was always too messed up to do it himself anyway.

There were two things that Dave was never caught without, a big wad of cash and a small metal briefcase.

The rather plain looking case was perpetually packed to the brim with an assortment of illegal drugs. He sold everything from special K to ecstasy.

I would have approximated the street value of the case's contents to be about $25.0000 and I always told him that it was crazy to bring it everywhere he went.

Dave was just like that though, ignorantly reckless. He drove his car with one knee on the steering wheel and both hands on a crack pipe. He never slept or ate. When he inevitably got popped, it came as no big surprise to me.

Another night I saw a man get stabbed in the front hall of the bar while I was on the phone. It happened right in front a crowd of people.

When the cops arrived someone pointed me out as a witness and I had to give them a fake name and number.

That was the last thing I needed to get involved in.

I stayed at Hanrahan's until I finally managed to convince one of my clients to rent an apartment in downtown Toronto. Marc and I moved in immediately and as you can imagine, this arrangement only lasted a few months, but at least I had made it to the big city.

Few things in life ever live up to their reputation but Hanrahan's was the exception. I've never seen such honest, in-your-face lawlessness as rampant and undisputed as it was there. It was also the only strip club that ever allowed me to wear my twenty-hole steel toe Doc's on stage. To me, Hanrahan's was home.

18
Unhappy Birthday

My twentieth birthday was approaching fast and as usual my life was a mess. I had recently moved out of the Riotstar party house and was living with Marc in Sue and Jelly's basement. I had left the house on Paradise Rd. mainly because my dealer lived upstairs and I was doing way too much blow. Jelly was getting clean and I though that theirs would be a good atmosphere to be around.

Most nights (when I wasn't working) we'd sit out on the porch smoking weed and jamming acoustically. Despite my feeble attempts however, I wasn't doing any less drugs. I was still dancing at Hanrahan's and there was always a constant flow of chemicals there. I was getting really fed up with Marc for being so useless and permanently unemployed and other than acquiring a small yet devoted fan base, my band was getting nowhere.

I saw it as a milestone year. I was a point in my life where I had to decide what I was going to do for the next decade, for what I thought was going to be the best times of my life. However, my advancing birthday was not the only reason that I was at a crossroads. I was waking up sick.

Each morning became a race from my bed to the bathroom where I'd crouch on the floor throwing up for hours. I was pregnant. At the time I was using so many hard drugs that I stopped having regular periods.

I'd get them sporadically every two or three months. By the time I realized that I was knocked up, I had already done so much that the damage would have been irreparable.

While my choices were simple, it was the hardest decision I have ever had to make. I knew either way I was never going to be the same.

Things were not looking very promising. As a high school drop out and drug addicted stripper, I wondered what kind of future I had to offer a baby. It also didn't help that I was no longer in love with Marc and I could just see myself having to harass him for diaper money.

He couldn't even afford to feed himself, let alone a baby. It was all so overwhelming. I made myself a promise. I decided that if I had an abortion, I would completely dedicate my life to my musical career. If I could somehow make a success of my band, then maybe my choice would eventually feel justifiable. Still, having an abortion would be like murdering a part of myself.

Some people believe that having the operation is a selfish act. I disagree. I think that bringing a child into an overcrowded, hateful world simply because you want to can be self-centered. I can remember being twelve years old and asking my parents why they created me. I resented them for giving me a life that I hated. After mentally struggling for days, I finally called the hospital and they booked me an appointment for August 11 (my birthday).

For weeks following the operation I was inconsolable. I felt like they had sliced away a part of my soul and left me hollow. It wasn't regret so much as self-hatred and shame.

It took all my strength to turn the pain into determination and from that moment on, I swore that the life I destroyed would not be in vain.

It was time to get serious, to tear myself open and expose my passion and rage. It became my responsibility to lay it all out on the line and to make my own destiny.

Over the next few years my band grew to be quite successful and as much as it wounded me, I grew to believe that I made the right choice.

Unfortunately, the emotional scars and the emptiness left behind by the abortion remain untouchable to this day and I stay forever unforgiven.

It was the worst birthday of my life.

19
The Sleezmobile

Another one of the crazy characters that I met while working at Hanrahan's, was a guy named Ted. Ted was a dealer who sold mainly coke, freebase and weed.

Most of the time I would give him private dances in exchange for drugs, which was my own way of cutting out the middle man and saving time. He was a guitar player and sometimes I would spend an entire shift with him just sitting at the bar talking about rock n' roll.

Ted was around thirty-five years old and had long wavy black hair. You could tell that he was in his prime during the eighties because he still dressed like an aging headbanger. He always wore ripped acid-wash jeans that looked about two sizes too small, dirty running shoes, and a tattered jean vest underneath a faded old biker jacket.

Basically, he was a white trash fashion disaster, but he had a great sense of humour and the best quality of drugs that I could find at the club.

Back then, I was completely clueless when it came to cars. A few months earlier I had bought my very first set of wheels and without realizing it, I had driven it dry.

Nobody told me that I had to add oil every now and again. Anyway, I was at the club one night and I happened to mention my predicament (a busted vehicle and no cash) to Ted. After having a good laugh at my expense, he told me that he had an old gutted van which he would gladly give to me, providing I put in the time to fix it up.

My eyes lit up as I imagined driving my band to all of our out of town shows in my very own Sleezmobile.

He told me that I could go over and check it out the next day. Although Ted had been one of my regular clients for several months, he had yet to fully gain my trust. I wasn't about to go over there alone, so I brought along my boyfriend Marc. Ted lived in Hamilton's east end, in a garage behind his grandmother's house.

The only access to the garage was through an alleyway that ran behind the houses. The overgrown pathway was filled with scraped vehicles, busted up furniture and piles of trash. Ted had planted weed along the full length of the alley which was easy to spot despite the heaps of discarded clutter. To me, it looked like the place where possessions must have gone to die.

Making our way to the front door of the shed was like crossing an obstacle course set in a junk yard.

After a couple of loud knocks, Ted opened the door to greet us. He held a smoking crack pipe in one hand and an open can of beer in the other. An outdated AC/DC album was blaring from the small stereo inside. There were a handful of people there parting with him, which he introduced us each to in turn. I looked at my watch and realized that it was still only ten o'clock in the morning. These were my kind of people. Go hard or go home!

Marc and I had a few tokes and each accepted a beer when he offered them to us. I was almost afraid to ask which one of the broken down vehicles out back was the one that he had told me about.

I reminded myself that whichever one it was, it was going to be free, and hesitantly asked him to show it to us.

Ted led us back behind the crack shack (which was what I called the garage), and then took us further down the narrow alley. I couldn't help but laugh when I finally saw it. Considering the cause of death of my first vehicle, he must have been out of his mind to think that I might have the capacity to fix up this piece of crap.

The van sat lopsided on the grass with only one wheel remaining. It was covered with gaping holes where the rust had rotted straight through the steel. There were no headlights, no seatbelts, no locks, and no handles to roll down the windows. Ted told me that the heater didn't work and of course, neither did the air conditioning. The gas gauge was busted and the alignment was totally screwed. In addition to all of this, it also needed a new carburetor, an alternator, a muffler and a new battery. There was no stereo and there were no backseats because the van had been previously disembowelled. I had no idea what most of these parts were, let alone how to replace them and unfortunately Marc knew even less about cars than I did. I explained all this to Ted and he offered his much needed assistance. It took me a few days to think about it, but in the end I couldn't deny that the price was right.

I managed to sell my old car (as is) for just under a thousand dollars. I knew that I had ripped the guy off, but I really needed the cash, and besides, I was planning to move to Toronto soon anyway.

He would have had a hell of a time trying to track me down for a refund. I found most of the parts that I needed used, and blew the rest of the money on dope.

I spent the entire summer of that year fixing up the van. Ted taught me how to camouflage most of the holes with bondo and cardboard and after scrubbing it down we put a plywood floor in the back. I got a bunch of carpet scraps for free, and used them to line and insulate the interior.

After I had finished grinding and sanding, I covered the exterior of the van with primer and set about making it a work of art. My plan was to turn it into an evil looking, psychedelic band wagon; something worthy of being called "The Sleezmobile".

Fortunately, I have always been blessed with the talent for both music and art, but it was obvious to me that airbrushing the entire van would be much more than a one woman job. So I did what I always do, I enlisted the help of those around me. TR was playing guitar for me at the time and turned out to be an amazing artist. He came over and covered the windowless back doors with a couple of skeletons that were drinking martinis.

Ted added a hot pink flame job to the front end of the van, and those members of the band that felt they couldn't draw very well, would help by filling things in with colour.

When we were finally finished, the van looked wilder than I had originally hoped. There were half-naked devil women, a skull and crossbones, a flaming guitar, and a heart with a dagger in it. There was also an iron cross, an anarchy symbol, an upside down pentagram, a silver jute box and several other universal symbols for hard rock.

Any spaces that might have been left blank were filled with music notes, tattoo style roses and stars covered with gold glitter. On each side of the van (where a company might display its name and logo), was a giant set of red lips with the words "CJ Sleez and the S.T.D's" scrawled across them. It looked utterly insane. I was so proud.

On the last day before I left Hamilton, I went over to Ted's place to pick up the Sleezmobile. He gave me one of his old license plates to use until I could get my own, an ounce of home-grown weed (which had recently been harvested from the alley behind the crack shack), and a small bag of cocaine. I was moving into one of Toronto's notoriously bad neighbourhoods, and so Ted also lent me his .22 calibre pistol and a handful of bullets.

Due to the big move, I had neither the time nor the money to legalize the van before using it. I didn't bother to get an emissions test, nor did I get a safety certificate, which of course meant that I had no insurance or legal papers. I had no proof of ownership and no registration card, so I put on the old license plate that Ted had given to me, and decided that it would have to due until I got myself settled in the new city.

Once in Toronto, the first major problem with the Sleezmobile was the non-existent door locks. Within a week some street scum prick had discovered the lack of locks and proceeded to turn the vehicle into his own little night-time home. Each morning I would head out to my parking spot with the gun loaded, ready for a confrontation.

Although I never caught the bum (as he was always gone long before dawn), the filthy fucker was always thoughtful enough to leave little surprise gifts behind for me to find. Some of the small tokens of his appreciation included used condoms, shattered glass crack pipes, mason jars full of urine, old newspapers, and everything else completely disgusting that a street lunatic would no longer consider useful. The ultimate surprise was when I awoke one morning only to uncover a big load of human feces waiting for me in the back of the van.

After saturating the carpet with three giant bottles of bleach, I took the Sleezmobile over to the local carwash.

There was absolutely no way that I was going to get down on my hands and knees to scrub that out. I picked up the sterilized van a few days later and was on my way home, wondering what the best way to get rid of the thing would be, when a cop pulled me over.

Shit, I thought. This thing is cursed!

The cop nailed me for everything he could; speeding, driving without valid license plates, driving in an unregistered vehicle and driving without insurance.

He even gave me a ticket for having an expired driver's license. It was only dumb luck that he didn't search me or he could have added possession to my long list of offences.

When he handed me a court date that was the final blow, I was totally fed-up. The Sleezmobile had turned out to be way more of a hassle than it was worth, which as you know, was nothing. I drove it out to my parents place and parked it in the backyard where it sat for almost two years.

After that, I gave it to my brother-in-law who used it to drive in the Ancaster fair's annual smash up derby. He didn't win, but the Sleezmobile put up a hell of a fight.

20
The Elmocambo

The Elmo was one of the few real Canadian rock n' roll landmarks. A huge neon palm tree ran along the exposed length of the three story building. The interior décor was eclectic and wore the bruises of many generations of great rock shows. The Elmo was famous mostly because it's where the Rolling Stone's played, but over the decades it had harboured bands from all over the world.

I can still recall how excited I was the first time I managed to book my band on a terrible Tuesday night time-slot. It was the first bar I played in Toronto and after a while (once I had paid my dues) and gained a fan base, I was able to headline on Friday and Saturday night.

The club was run by Dan Burke. He was the promoter/booking agent and was also famous in his own right (mostly for his wild, out of control antics).

Dan lived illegally in the office on the third floor.

There was no kitchen or shower but there was a couch when he needed it. For the first few years that I lived in Toronto it was my second home.

I worked with him at the club for some time and we shared an equal appetite for self-destruction. Dan showed enthusiastic support for my musical career from the very beginning, and it was Dan who initially set me up with Stacy Stray. Stacy and I nicknamed him "Parky" because of his constant trips to "Moss Park" to score rock. With Parky at the helm, the Elmo was nothing but a ticking time bomb.

One night "Teenage Head" was playing on the second floor and the room was packed to capacity. Stacy and I always drank for free and were completely smashed as usual. I had already known the band back from when I lived in Hamilton. In fact they were at the first gig that I ever played. Anyway, I was dancing at the side of the stage and I had to go to the washroom (five or ten beers have a tendency to do that) and it was so crowded that I had already been holding it for some time. The space between the stage and the ladies room seemed impenetrable. When I told Stacy, he looked at the mass of people and shook his head in disbelief.

"Why don't you just go here?"

"What?"

"C'mon", he said scooping me up onto his shoulders. I screamed in drunken delight.

"Go ahead, I dare you". He knew that those were the three magic words I've never been able to resist. So I did it. I took a leak right there. We were both soaking wet and laughing hysterically. Stacy was always able to make me laugh.

I hopped back down and started dancing again. Steve (the bass player) motioned for me to come up and dance beside him on the edge of the stage. I had just climbed up there and started to shake it, when some macho jerk-off from the crowd ran up and ripped my tiny gold tube-dress down around my knees. There I was, on stage at someone else's show, drenched in my own pee and wearing nothing but a black satin g-string and a pair of stiletto heels.

I was so pissed off! I pulled my dress back up and dove into the crowd fists a-flailing. I was so bombed however; that I completely missed the moronic troublemaker and accidentally slugged his almost-innocent friend (he was still guilty by association as far as I was concerned).

Just as the brawl began to spread through the crowd Stacy yanked me back to the bar for more beers.

I found out later from a friend that the assholes at the front of the stage were off-duty cops. Wow, Big shock!

What a bunch of sexually repressed losers, I thought. I'm still looking forward to the day that I see cops serve and protect anyone but themselves. They're just like a giant gang of squares.

The Elmo was also the venue of my birthday bash for three consecutive years. My parties were over-the-top and always made great press. It was only a matter of time before the entire room and its occupants would be covered in chocolate cake and campaign. Playing live has always been my favourite thing to do. I still wish for it every year.

Another night Parky and I put together a Jimi Hendrix tribute show. This was just one of a string of cover song nights that we did including The Rolling Stones, Led Zeppelin, and Guns n' Roses. Each time the tunes would be played by hot local musicians and there was always a great turn-out. This particular night was different because for me, it symbolized the beginning of the end of the Elmo.

By the time Stacy and I arrived at the club (fashionably late as always) Parky was psychotically drunk. I was greeted at the backstage door with a barrage of obscene insults. The room was filled with artists and gossiping scenesters who all fell silent and stared at us.

I was taken completely off guard and instinctively responded in kind. This was too much for Parky to take.

He dropped to the floor, clung to my leg and burst into tears. I tried to shake him off and called to his girlfriend asking for the assistance that she never did offer.

I was so embarrassed. With each squirming step I took he tightened his grip until I was backed into a corner.

Then he stood up and tried to kiss me. For Stacy this was the final straw. He pulled Parky off me and pushed him up against the wall questioning him angrily. I took the opportunity to slip away and escaped back to the main bar where I swung back some shots and composed myself.

Five minutes later though, they both joined me and the situation once again began to escalate.

I decided then that the best thing we could do was leave.

Later that night we got a phone call from Steve Saint. He told me that after we had left the bar, things had gotten progressively worse. Parky had gotten himself involved in a big scrap in front of the club after closing time.

The doorman found him unconscious and bleeding on the sidewalk. They called an ambulance and now he was at the hospital in intensive care. Stacy and I got dressed and met Saint in the emergency room.

We walked in and Dan was lying there motionless and utterly unresponsive. His head was incredibly swollen and he was missing some teeth. I walked over and held his hand. Recognizing my voice he opened his eyes, sat up and started rambling off a slew of incoherent babble.

To be honest, that was the part that freaked me out.

Within a week Parky was back in his cluttered office and back to his usual questionable antics. For me however, things at the Elmo were never quite the same.

Parky's erratic behaviour was not enjoyed by all, and after a while he inevitably burned a few bridges. He broke up with his girlfriend and started spending a lot more time in the park. Despite the incompetence of the staff, it came as a shock when I learned that the building had been sold and was being converted into a dance studio.

The Elmo's days of rock n' roll were numbered.

The community pulled together in an attempt to stop the change. We held demonstrations, signed petitions; we even met with our local congressman. It was all useless.

On the last night it was open, the Elmocambo became a free-for-all. Everyone was drunk and ripping the bar apart, either out of spite or simply for the sake of stealing a souvenir. It was after all, the end of an era.

Five years later the Elmo once again changed ownership and was re-opened as a rock club.

Most of us were still jaded after the initial closure and I never went back. It just wouldn't have felt right.

21
Fleur Du Mal

I had been a fan of "the Viletones" since my early days as a punk. Steven Leckie was their infamous lead singer.

He was the one responsible for turning "the Last Pogo" into a riotous blood bath. Leckie was the original self-mutilating angst filled teen. He was a friend to Sid and Nancy, an associate to Malcolm McLaren and a distinguished veteran of the punk movement.

One night, Dan Burke invited me to an art opening at the "Fleur Du Mal" gallery which was owned and operated by Leckie. It was an offer that I couldn't refuse.

I arrived at the Elmo to pick up Parky and found him in his third floor office. He was seated behind his desk, which was piled high with toppling papers and promotional band swag. He smiled and nodded when he saw me, but had both his hands full (one hand holding the phone, the other a smoking crack pipe). Several large lines of cocaine were laid out sloppily in front of him. He took another hit off the pipe, hung up the phone and pointed to the piles of white powder offering me some. What a wonderful muti-tasker, I thought. This was Parky at his best.

Fleur Du Mal was on the corner of Queen and Sherburne, an area that was notorious in Toronto.

On one of the other corners there was a homeless shelter, on another was "Moss Park" where bums slept on benches and schizophrenics wandered around in circles mumbling to themselves. On the last corner there was a dingy little coffee shop. I ordered a pop once from the tiny oriental woman behind the counter and I can remember thinking that she had the worst job in the world. I appropriately nicknamed the place "Crackton."

In sharp contrast to its surroundings, the interior of Fleur Du Mal was impressive.

The long narrow gallery was painted bone white from floor to ceiling. The only notable colours in the room were those of the art, which was hung meticulously from every wall. There were two totally nude people (a woman and a man) that had been body-painted, each in their own ornate design. Each held two silver trays filled with elegant looking hors d'oeuvres. It was all very hip.

Leckie was behind the counter at the rear of the room, passing out red wine and Champaign.

He had a shaved head, a goatee and was covered in poorly done tattoos (jail tats I call them).

Leckie looked great for a guy his age and reminded me of a thin Anton Lavey. At least, Steve looked equally as evil. I asked him for his autograph and his eyes lit up.

He jumped at the chance to have his ego stroked by a hot young chick. After pouring me a drink, he took my hand and led me on an exclusive tour of the exhibit.

We proudly sauntered around the room, briefly stopping to greet each guest in succession. Leckie remained the perfect gentleman as he politely introduced me to everyone. On our way down to the lower level, I noticed that the walls of the stairwell were decorated with framed newspaper clippings of Leckie himself, dating back from 1978 to the present. Obviously he took full advantage of his social status and reputation amongst Toronto's' rock n' roll crowd. Parky and I stayed at the gallery until the wee hours of the morning and before I left I gave Leckie my number.

I had just moved to Toronto with Marc and I knew he would get a kick out of meeting him.

He called me a few days later and I went over to hang out after the gallery closed. This time I brought Marc with me. Leckie liked Marc immediately and told him he was like a younger version of himself. We had a blast! Literally. We spent the entire visit sitting around smoking crack.

It was probably because of the buzz, but the conversation never lost its pace and before we realized it, it was after midnight.

"We should get going", I said as I pulled on my heavy boots. "If we don't leave now we'll be here all night."

"Sure, but let me walk you to a cab. It's a bad neighbourhood", said Steve. I smirked and put on my coat, (little did he know, we lived only two blocks away).

We got about three steps out the door before we were approached by a nasty black guy who wanted to sell us more rock. We shrugged him off and flagged a taxi.

Walking around that intersection at night was never fun.

On my twenty-second birthday, I played at The Elmo.

After the show, Steve Leckie came backstage to see me. It was the first time he had seen me perform and he was blown away.

He took off his iron cross necklace, gave it to me and told me that he was passing on the torch.

I recognized it immediately from the photos on the early Viletones albums. I was honoured.

Shortly thereafter, Steve introduced me to Jan Houst who ran an independent record label called "Other People's Music."

Some of his releases included Iggy Pop, Dee Dee Ramone, Teenage Head, the Forgotten Rebels, the Sinisters, and the Viletones.

Jan and I hit it off fabulously and in the spring of 2001 my first album ("Rock Action") was released on OPM.

Within the year, Leckie had dropped out of the scene completely and Fleur Du Mal was no more.

Rumours circulated that he had gone back to rehab, but I never got the full story.

22
Stacy Stray

I can't recall the first time I ever met Stacy Stray. I had seen him around several times at the local rock clubs, but it wasn't until he graced the cover of the NXNE music festival guide that I was impressed enough to make him mine. He was playing lead guitar in Robin Black and the Intergalactic Rockstars, who were one of the hottest bands in Toronto at the time.

Parky was a mutual friend and one night while we were drinking at the Bovine Sex Club, Stacy joined the two of us. The Bovine was one of the hottest hard rock bars in Toronto and was another one of my usual haunts.

Stacy and I hit it off immediately. I found him incredibly charming and entertaining. The three of us had so much fun at the bar, that when it closed for the night we continued the party at a local booze can, then later at my apartment. Stacy was shocked to find a girl that could keep up with his heavy drinking and was amazed at my energy and tolerance for drugs. We were a perfect match.

That's how it was in the beginning, long nights filled with liquor and laughter. For the first couple of weeks we were never alone. We were always surrounded by friends or band members and it wasn't until months later that I found out the real reason why. Apparently, Stacy was afraid to have a private night with me because he knew we'd end up sleeping together and he was terrified of falling in love with me. Not only did he not want a girlfriend, but once again my reputation had preceded me and he had heard that I was trouble.

During the day Stacy worked as a hairstylist downtown at a posh salon and his strong feminine side was just enough to compliment my aggressive tendencies. I had him play on 'Rock Action' (my first record) as a session musician, and was blown away by his style and skill with a guitar. I knew then that it was only a matter of time before I would seduce him into leaving his band to join mine.

After dating exclusively for three months, I moved in with him into his tiny cockroach infested bachelor apartment located in Toronto's downtown arts district.

He had lived there for almost seven years and over time had grown accustomed to the filth and infestation.

I on the other hand, lasted only a few short months before finding us a suitable studio space a few blocks away.

Stacy was always weird like that, he avoided nice things because he said he didn't want to get used to the comfort and then have to go without while he was away on tour.

I never understood his twisted logic in that respect as I enjoy everything I can for as long as possible. I do agree however, that in enough time you can get used to anything.

Although we were madly in love, it wasn't always roses with us. While the sex was totally intense, so were the fights. Of course it didn't help that we went out drinking together almost every night.

On one occasion we were so wasted and were scrapping so bad that I pulled out my .22 calibre pistol just to shut him up. He started daring me to shoot him and finally I aimed the gun over his head and pulled the trigger.

The bullet went straight through the window and left a perfect little hole in the Plexiglas as a reminder of the argument. A few months later I sold the gun to one of my friends in the Hell's Angels. I'm sure if I didn't one or both of us would be dead by now. Psychotic bitches and guns don't exactly make a good combination.

I blame myself for bringing heroin into the house.

One of my girlfriends was a stripper named Siren and whenever I ran into her at work she would give me lines of the stuff. I can honestly say (without pride) that I've never turned down an offer to do free drugs.

It started off innocent enough (or at least as sinless as it gets for me), but before long I was buying my own supply and bringing it home.

Stacy did a lot of touring during those first few years that we were together and I don't think he realized how bad my addiction had become until he came back one day and I was using needles again.

Stacy was my third serious relationship with a guy and if there's one thing I'd learned, it was that when men fall for me, they fall hard. So, rather than take a stand and leave me, Stacy chose to join me. What I mean is that he put up a weak resistance until I tied him off and gave him his first shot. I now know that was the beginning of our end, but at the time it seemed like just another sacrifice that he had made in order to be with me.

Within a few weeks Stacy was just as hooked on heroin as I was and the two of us were burning through hundreds of dollars worth of dope each day.

We managed to maintain our insane lifestyle for almost a year. We were poor as hell, but we were also usually high which made everything else seem irrelevant.

It wasn't until we went to visit my parents for Christmas that everything fell apart. I had scored enough dope to last us a few days so that we could stay over and still be comfortable. The only problem was that we were such a couple of fiends, that within hours of arriving the entire stash was gone. As a result, by the time everybody in my family sat down for Christmas dinner, Stacy and I were undeniably junk sick. It was so brutally obvious. Our addiction had become too hard to hide. My parents were actually really cool about the whole situation. They offered to put us both up while we got off the stuff and into a methadone program. At the time we were losing our apartment anyway, so Stacy and I moved out of Toronto and (temporarily) back to Hamilton.

The moment that we moved in with my parents, we stopped making love. The shame, guilt and discomfort of coming down off drugs was enough to drive any couple apart, even one as passionate as Stacy and I. At first I was the only one on the methadone program.

For three months Stacy remained in denial and insisted that he was strong enough to kick the habit on his own. However, I knew better and suspected he was still using behind my back. It didn't take long for me to prove it either, as the first time I searched through his stuff, I found his secret stash. We were both furious with each other.

I told him he could either sign up for the program or move out. He stayed with me but it was never the same after that. He had lost my trust and was filled with resentment. I'm not saying that I was a complete success on methadone, far from it. I had several relapses and it's still a daily struggle. That fight just made me realize that we were no longer in it together.

There truly is a fine line between love and hate, and after a year of scrapping with no make-up sex, we were just about ready to kill each other. I couldn't stand the constant bickering and eventually broke it off. We had been together for four years. I think once a relationship gets to a certain point and there are more bad memories than good, there's no turning back. We had simply been through too much together. The romance had died and we had become more like a brother and sister than the lovers we once were.

Stacy and I both agreed that the band should come before any personal problems and so we made the commitment to continue playing together. It was one of the hardest adjustments I've ever had to make but in the end it was worth it. I still have yet to meet a better guitar player.

23
Temptress

In the spring of '99 I received a call from my Parky. The Boston based drag queen act Temptress was coming to Toronto to play the annual NXNE music festival and they were looking for a couple of girls to dress up in sexy clothes and sing back-ups with them.

Parky had immediately thought of me. I had never heard of the group before and was not quite sure what to expect. Although I was playing the same weekend with my own band, I refused to turn down an opportunity to make money playing music so I signed up for the gig.

I contacted the lead singer Chucky and asked him to mail me a press kit along with a couple of CDs. Once I had a chance to listen to it, I found the music derivative of the New York Dolls and Jane County.

It was a style I was familiar with and managed to learn the material within a few short days.

I still needed to find another girl to join the show. The job was after all, for two of us. I immediately thought of my friend Sue. We sang together before in the High School Hookers and still had some matching costumes we could use. She enthusiastically accepted and arranged to meet us at the club before the show. We were both professionals and were confident despite the absence of rehearsals. Besides, it wasn't our name on the poster.

It wasn't long before the weekend of the festival arrived. Chucky phoned me from the hotel after settling in. I graciously accepted his invitation to meet for drinks and get better acquainted. My first impression of him was that of a downtrodden, unattractive middle aged woman.

His long wispy hair appeared to be in the process of slowly recovering from a bad home perm.

He wore an over-sized 'Looney Tunes' golf shirt which was tucked into a pair of high waisted jeans. Overall, I had a hard time believing he was straight, which of course he claimed to be. But really, I mean why else would any man wear rubber breasts and high heels?

During the day Chucky worked for a communications company and made a handsome salary. In his spare time he transformed into the only real member of Temptress.

All the other musicians (including myself) were paid to play on a show by show basis. At this time the band consisted of four enormous black guys from the Bronx. Normally they were committed to their own group which was called The Piranha Bros.

After briefly getting to know each other at the hotel bar, we hailed three cabs and headed towards the venue.

Despite his bloated figure, Chucky made an amazing drag queen once he was dressed up in full make-up and wearing his big bouffant wig. We hit the stage with a bang but before long the entire room was laughing. It was simply unavoidable. Chucky's voice was unbearable.

He couldn't land a note to save his life. It was painfully clear to me then why Sue and I were hired, not to mention the four enormous guys beside us. It was to drown him out. The audience needed as many distractions as they could get. My only consolation was that I was also laughing.

We closed the set with a song called "Crack the Whip". As part of the grand finale Sue and I pulled a couple of guys from the crowd onto the stage with us, then bent them over and whipped them. It was totally hilarious. After the show we all went to watch Robin Black play at Lee's Palace. To my pleasant surprise Chucky remained in full drag for the rest of the festival, even though his gig was over on the first night.

He definitely made a better looking woman than a man.

After NXNE, Chucky and I remained long distance friends. On two separate occasions he flew Sue and I down to the States for more work. The first trip was to Boston where he was recording his second album entitled "Odd Squad". At first we had a great time and were given the full rock star treatment, all expenses paid plus a generous cheque. It wasn't until we were in the studio and Chucky started recording his vocals that I felt like I was earning the money. We spent three full days held up there while he tried to finish the vocals on one track. It was agonizing.

The photo shoot for the album cover also took place during that trip. Sue and I had both sent our measurements ahead of time, but when the costumes arrived, the seamstress had mixed up our waist measurements with our hips. The result was pants that barely fit over our thighs and couldn't be zipped up. To top it all, I had to wear a black afro wig which is something I'll never do again.

On the brighter side, our visit coincided with the Boston Arts Festival. I insisted we take a day off to go see the sights and wander along Mulberry St. After the studio and photos we needed a day off to become friends again.

Our third Temptress gig was the Greenwich Village Halloween Parade. We arrived early and were able to spend the better part of the week exploring Manhattan.

Sue and I shared a room at the Downtown Holiday Inn and we rehearsed with the rest of the band in one of Madonna's old jam spaces. Performing at the parade was one of my all time favourite gigs.

Chucky had prepared a "Rock the Vote" float and had us all dress up in stars and stripes.

This time I sewed my own costume and it fit me perfect. The streets were tightly packed with outlandish costumes.

Ghosts, ghouls, witches, cartoons and everything else imaginable could be spotted in the sea of faces. For the first time, Chucky fit right in.

There were so many spectators, even the windows of the buildings that lined the street seemed to spill over with those struggling to catch a glimpse of the event.

Once the float was in motion, we sang two songs over and over while tossing hundreds of Temptress CDs into the cheering crowd.

I was jumping around so much that by the end of the parade route I was drenched in sweat, which quickly froze to my skin when we stopped to unload. Cold, stiff and tired, Sue and I stumbled back to the hotel in our four inch stilettos. It was the best Halloween ever!

The last show I played with Temptress was in Toronto at the Bovine Sex Club the following year.

Chucky had rented an RV and drove up with the rest of the band. Due to the set up of the bar, it was impossible for Sue and I to change clothes between songs in their washroom. The crowd was simply too thick. Instead, Chucky parked the RV out front and we had to race between the two. The distance made us late for every song and in the mad rush we both wiped out several times. Chucky's voice had noticeably deteriorated over the past year and had hit an all new low. The show was a disaster and left me feeling angry and embarrassed.

I had been working hard pushing my own band in T.O. and after that show; I finally decided that singing behind Chucky in that side show was damaging my reputation.

Like so many other bands, somewhere along the way it just stopped being fun. After that night I never saw him again. We left each other on a friendly note and overall, singing with Temptress was a great experience.

In the end, I guess I just outgrew it.

24
California Christmas

It was the second last week of 2001.

That fall, I had been seduced into signing a two year contract with a so-called "hot shot" manager from L.A.

Stacy and I were flying to California for the holidays to meet him and crash at his bungalow for a couple of weeks to comprise a plan of promotional attack.

He had even been recommended to me by Jan.

This guy was a real smooth talker who had been courting me over the phone for weeks.

As a result, lawyers had been hired and papers had been signed before we'd even met each other in person.

Optimistically, I was hoping that my career might get a jump start.

Realistically, I was happy for the break from the dismal anticipation of a long, cold Canadian winter.

Stacy and I arrived at LAX airport only to discover our new manager had not shown up to pick us up, I checked my phone messages and discovered our host had decided to take a very last minute trip to Vegas and had no intention of returning to L.A. anytime during our stay. I contacted my record label back in Canada and explained the situation.

Thankfully they pulled through and wired me five hundred American dollars.

That was just enough for a week's rent in a cheap motel, booze and a daily fast-food fix.

We took a cab to the most shameless retreat in West Hollywood, the cheapest one in the phone book, the Sunset Palms Motel.

Still, it was nicer than the one room roach infested mess that Stacy and I shared during the first eight months of our turbulent love affair.

The first couple of nights we explored the customary strip of cliché rock clubs; the Whiskey, the Viper Room, the House of Blues, etc.

During the day I wandered up and down Melrose visiting all the trendy clothing stores. Basically, we tried to make the most of it.

The Spanish magazine "Popular 1" had arranged to interview us while we were down there.

Their idea was to team up CJ Sleez with Texas Terri for a shared spread. I met Terri for the first time on Christmas Eve.

Before we even left the motel we were calling each other "big" and "lil" sis, (I was designated the latter of the two).

"Bubble" was playing at the Dragonfly and Terri wanted to introduce me to her friend Share.

Share was the former bassist of the all girl 80's metal band Vixen, a veteran of the L.A. scene and was now the lead singer of "Bubble."

Despite the flakey band name, she was super cool and after a drink or three, I was on stage singing with her.

The next afternoon, in true Rockstar fashion, we did the scheduled interview from our motel bed.

It was the third day of our trip and Stacy and I were now smack dab in the middle of withdrawal.

I had hoped to score some smack while down there but all I could find fast enough was weed.

We were both drinking non-stop to try to dull the unyielding ache. When you're that sick, a hangover feels like a blessing.

Before we lost the sun to the horizon, I pulled myself together to take the pictures required for the magazine article. I suggested that we walk down to the local strip club and shoot the photos there.

On the way, I jumped into a migrant shopping cart and Terri pushed me down the sloping hill running behind me to keep up.

We loitered at the club for a couple more beers before saying our good-byes.

The next day Stacy went out and got a tattoo that he had previously asked me to draw for him.

It was a big red heart, pierced with a black music note and wrapped in a banner that said "SLEEZ."

We ate our Christmas dinner at Kenny Roger's Roasters and spent Christmas day watching a movie at Graumann's Chinese Theatre.

After the film we found an open supermarket and treated ourselves to champagne and strawberries.

I love that in the States you can buy liquor at the grocery store. Even on Christmas day!

In the end, our once ill-fated adventure turned out to be one of my most memorable Christmases.

As for the manager, I never spoke to him again.

25
Prisoner

It isn't long before the sickness and the desperation sets in.

The chilling inescapable pain quickly tightens its grip.

Your body freezes from the inside out and every ounce of your weight multiples around you like a sponge soaking in molasses.

Absolute solitude penetrates you as it becomes agonizingly obvious how utterly alone you are, and will be, now left with the consequences of your own impending hell.

The rotten veins beneath your skin shrink like salt on a slug, burning and screaming out.

Sweat coats your clammy flesh like a crude oil slick.

Your mind speeds out of control as thunderous chaotic thoughts thrash at your sanity.

You try to sleep but there's no point, the cramps won't allow it.

Your guts twist and gnaw away at themselves and you struggle to catch your breath.

Hot, toxic fluids are expelled from every orifice.

Your eyes fill with tears that soon spill over and splash down your cheeks, leaving that familiar salty taste on your lips.

There's no comfort in weakness though, there never is.

You're a condemned prisoner, forced to suffer a full sentence because good behaviour no longer applies.

It lasts for days, sometimes weeks and you can be sure that when it's all over, you'd do it again in a second.

Drug addiction is like a curse.

You watch your whole world gradually disintegrate around you.

Everything you own and everyone you know eventually gets thrown away.

The rest of your life is spent trying to pull the pieces back together and reclaim those things that you have lost.

It never works though. You can't take it back.

Addiction is the endless game of catching up with yourself, of struggling to keep your head above water and of striving to keep your name relevant when nobody cares anymore.

It is a tiresome, heartbreaking cycle that will not be stopped.

It's attempting to exist in a world that hates you right back and it's always searching for a justification that never comes.

26
No Sleep 'till Lisbon
CJ Sleez's first European Tour

As a young, independent artist working during the turn of the century, one of my greatest resources was the internet.

Our website (www.cjsleez.com) acted as a global advertisement for the band and I was now able to communicate with industry professionals that I otherwise wouldn't have had access to.

I was my own manager, booking agent, promoter and stylist, among other things. I had nothing to sell except myself, but I fully believed in the product.

One afternoon I was searching the internet for new contacts when I came across a small punk rock label from Spain called "Safety Pin Records."

Back then I was constantly shipping out free CD's in the hopes that somebody somewhere would show enough interest to work with me.

So, I sent them a press kit and a few weeks later Safety Pin e-mailed me back offering to press and distribute a version of the album in Spain, in exchange for a portion of whatever we decided to press. I was thrilled.

I sent them six songs off of "Rock Action" and suggested that they release it as a vinyl picture disk.

They pressed a thousand copies and sent me two hundred of them. About a month later I got another message from Safety Pin. This time they were offering to book a tour in Spain and Portugal to help promote and sell the record. I jumped at the chance and spent the next couple of weeks working out the details. I put together a solid five piece band for the tour that included Stacy, his best friends Neil and Rich, and a drummer I called Scooby. After lots of rehearsals and a few local shows we were ready to go.

We arrived at Pearson airport with just over two hours to kill before our scheduled departure.

It was during this time that I made one of the biggest mistakes of my life. I ate a chicken sandwich from an airport cafeteria. Never again! The plane had barely left the ground when I was overcome by the worst case of food poisoning I've ever had. I spent the entire flight vomiting on myself and by the time we landed in England for our lay-over, I was completely delirious.

Unable to walk to the next gate, I had to be helped by the guys, who put me in a luggage cart and wheeled me through the terminal.

When we reached the security check, the guards took one look at my green complexion and refused to let us through. Everything was falling apart and we hadn't even gotten there yet! Thankfully, after some passionate pleading and serious sweet talking, they eventually agreed to let us through on the condition that I could walk unassisted. I mustered every ounce of strength that I had left and attempted to fake some significant level of improvement. I dropped my leaking bag of vomit on the x-ray conveyor belt, staggered through the metal detectors, and then retrieved the dripping plastic sac just in time to make another contribution.

There was no way that I was going to miss that plane! Once we got to Portugal the guys realized that the airline had lost two of their guitars on the way. So far our "No Sleep 'till Lisbon" tour was biting the big one.

It took us two days to find a doctor that finally gave me a shot of Gravol in the ass. With my nausea slowly subsiding I was now free to catch up with the rest of the band. Stacy and Rich were both heavy drinkers, but Neil was on a pill kick. He spent the first week bouncing back between valium and speed until he became so ultra paranoid that we lost our driver.

What I mean is, that he quit because Neil wouldn't stop being a sketch, bitching about his speeding, constantly complaining, and whining that we were all going to crash. Our replacement driver calmed him down a bit, but he also managed to get us to every show late.

Festimad '02

We pulled into the outdoor stadium with five minutes to hit the stage. Frantically, I tore off my clothes in the back of the van and tied on a string bikini. The guys scrambled for their gear as I quickly teased my hair and put on some lipstick. It was absolute chaos. My bassist hadn't stopped drinking for about a week (to compensate for the pills), and at this point he could barley stand.

My extremely anal drummer broke out into another one of his temper tantrums, freaking out about the rush, (with him, everything always had to be just so). At several shows during the tour he actually nailed the drum kit to the stage to keep it from shifting away from him. His up-tight, straight edge attitude really had no place in the band and as soon as we got home I found a more compatible band member. Stacy and Rich set out in search of some suitable amps, as other than the guitars and bass (which were lost), we didn't bring any of own gear over to Europe.

A few minutes later we were backstage and ready to go.

On the way to centre stage we were intercepted by a barrage of photographers and press people. I politely asked them to come back after the show when we would have some more time to speak to them. Right now, it was time to play. Until I was standing in front of the massive crowd, I had no idea the number of people that attended Festimad each year. This was the big time. I looked out into a field of expectant faces. Thousands of music fans were anxiously waiting to find out what the little blonde Canadian girl was all about.

My heart pounded as I heard the first chords cut through the air and I pressed my palm against my chest as if to stop it from bursting through my ribcage and spilling out onto the stage floor. Overcome by the familiar rush of adrenaline, I took a long haul off my cigarette before dropping it at my feet and destroying it with my platform heel. I was one of the few remaining front people who actually smoked and sang at the same time.

"Are you ready to rock?" I screamed into the microphone coaxing the crowd and beckoning a hail of excited cheers. "Let's show 'em what we're made of boys."

The bass and drums bolted into action joining the thundering guitars. Together they formed a wall of sound that radiated straight through me and shook my bones. I started to sing, slapping the audience to attention.

I could feel the thousands of eyes on me as the crowd exploded like dynamite in a bonfire. The energy enveloped me, filling me with confidence and prideful power.

It was time to let myself loose upon the world again.

In perfect unison we continued to take the music higher, louder and harder. Filling the stadium with sound, our music drove the crowd into a frenzy of lost inhibitions. Sweat stung my eyes as I looked out into a mass of faces and writhing bodies squeezed shoulder to shoulder.

I shook from head to toe, singing from the depths of my soul, releasing the wrath of my insanity.

We burned through our final songs with the intensity of a sudden electrical storm. Finally, I blew a kiss to the crowd and the five of us left the stage together.

As soon as were got backstage we were handed 26'ers of Jack Daniel's and Tequila Gold. With the rest of the night off, I knew that things were going to get wild.

Stacy and I were then ushered into a large media tent to do some interviews on television, radio and internet broadcasts. We were well on our way to being wasted and during one of the interviews (hopefully the radio one), I was talking about how nice our Spanish fans were.

At every show we played people would come up to us and hand us free drugs. It was incredible! When I was asked what kind of drugs, I pulled out my tin cigarette case which contained weed, hash, coke and some heroin that I had managed to score in Madrid. I told him it was my Spanish tour survival kit. The DJ loved it.

It was the third week into the tour and tensions were running high. Combine that with an unlimited supply of drugs and alcohol and you can guess what happened next. After the interviews, Stacey and I stumbled backstage, each grasping a half empty bottle of alcohol, Stacy with his JD, me with my Cuervo. We found the rest of the band waiting for us with mutinous looks on the faces.

Well, we were all completely inebriated and belligerent, what better time for a band meeting right?

An open airing of grievances erupted amongst the band and ended in an all-out screaming match involving mainly my bass player and myself. Due to my intoxicated state, I can't remember exactly what he had said to make me throw my drink in his face, but it must have been pretty bad. This started a heinous chain reaction which resulted in an all-out band brawl. Soon we were all covered in booze, throwing punches and chasing each other around with empty bottles.

Our tour manager was the first one to receive the call that something was amiss, but by this point she had grown so accustomed to our outlandish antiques, that she waved it off as inconsequential and decided to work on her topless tan. We had become so out of control that I was later told that a member of the press had suspected that the whole scene had been staged.

After all, no one could actually be that crazy.

Barcelona

Barcelona was the most beautiful city that I've ever seen. It's also one of the very few places where you can buy authentic absinthe. Strolling through the gothic cobblestone streets adorned with intricately carved angels, demons and gargoyles, I felt like I was on the set of a classic horror film. I have never felt so inspired by a city. The ancient cathedrals and colossal water fountains surrounded us as we set out in search of an absinthe bar.

By the time we found the tiny shop, we had just enough time to down some shots, purchase a few bottles of absinthe and race over to the venue to do our sound check.

For some reason every Spanish band that opened for us ended up sucking big time. I couldn't figure out how an entire country was unable to play half decent rock n' roll.

The best that I could guess was that maybe their standards had been so low for so long that nobody ever had to bother getting really good. I mean in North America it's different because bands are a dime a dozen.

The competition forces us to improve. However, despite the Spaniards inept musical abilities, they were all incredibly cool people who were fully respectful of our hedonistic rock n' roll lifestyles. These bands may not have had the talent, but the attitude was there nonetheless.

One of the members of our opening band in Barcelona was an inventor. He had created his own "musical" instrument made out of human bones. It was about the size of a guitar and strung like a violin. The neck of the instrument was made of a thick white thigh bone and several ribs formed the lower half where the strings were stretched across the open underside of a smooth white skull. It was wonderfully grotesque. He "played" it balanced between his legs, similar to the stance of a cellist and it was the worst sound I've ever heard. Intolerably high pitch screeching and shrieking noises struggled to escape from the tormented strings. The morbid noise wasn't loud, but it was potent and completely distracting from the rest of the band. In the end, the instrument proved to be an insurmountable annoyance.

Their set was the worst of the entire tour and I was grateful when it was our turn to hit the stage.

When the show was over, we all dropped ecstasy (courtesy of the crazy opening band), and drove down to the beach. As soon as our van stopped on the boardwalk the back doors swung open and Stacy and Rich took off like a shot. As they ran towards the pitch black ocean they tore off their clothes piece by piece until all we could see was two pale white asses plunging into the water.

A few minutes later they joined the rest of us on the beach for some more absinthes. They were shivering and Rich had a small scratch on his chest that was slightly bleeding. I've never seen anybody cause such a fuss over such a pathetically unsubstantial little cut.

I suddenly understood why he was still a tattoo virgin.

We had to hear about it for the rest of the tour and every time a fan would take his picture, he would lift up his shirt to show off his non-existent wound. It was so embarrassing.

I guess he must have thought that it made him look tough and even when we started mocking him for it, calling him Sid Vicious he still didn't pick up on our sarcasm.

That night we had the entire Barcelona beach to ourselves.

The guys had brought along their guitars and a couple of portable battery powered amps and we stayed there drinking and playing together until the sun rose.

It was the best time I had on that tour.

27
Aftermath

It has been three weeks since the incident; yet, the haunting stench of death still lingers in the air.

The odour is unmistakable and circulates the vicinity, battling with low oxygen levels, dust and carbon dioxide for supremacy in the reluctant lungs of the city dwellers.

It is a scent that, I hope, I'll never have the displeasure of recognizing again, burnt flesh and fatality.

It is well past midnight but, is still glaringly bright outside, as the grounds are flooded with artificial lights.

Standing guard on the perimeter, massive steel girders curl themselves towards the earth like burnt matches.

Across the street, the entire side of a building is missing. It seems strange, but the remaining halves of the rooms are still intact, as if they had been sliced straight through the middle.

Then, unexpectedly, it starts to rain.

Unfazed by the downpour, emergency crews continue to painstakingly sift through the miniature mountains of rubble which are scattered in the place where the proud structures once stood.

An illogically optimistic looking ambulance colours the dismal destruction zone with its silent red siren. Paramedics are standing by.

I look towards the sky and let the rain mingle with my tears, cleansing my face. This is too much, even for me.

I turn and walk toward the subway. It will take much more than a rainstorm to heal this place.

28
Wilhelmina Waste-Case

I was working at a shady strip club in downtown Toronto's east end when Norwayne first introduced himself.

He was a conspicuously gay black guy who ran a modeling company a few blocks away. I was sceptical after meeting so much scum at the bars, such as people pretending to be something they're not in a pathetic attempt to impress me. Norwayne had to be stubborn. It wasn't until he returned to pester me for the third time that I actually sat down and took him seriously.

As a teenager I had looked into joining several modeling agencies but had been repeatedly discouraged when asked to pay an outrageous membership fee.

It was simply a luxury that I couldn't afford and my parents weren't interested in helping me out.

Therefore, I was on my own. I began the daunting task of compiling a book or photo resumé by working with student photographers and anyone else who was willing to work for free. Only about ten percent of the prints ended up being good enough to use, but over the next few years they slowly added up, as did my experience in front of a camera.

I became a freelance model and found work mainly wearing lingerie and leather fetish wear. With my tattoos and rock n' roll attitude, I had always assumed that the world of high fashion wouldn't be ready for the likes of me. Norwayne optimistically disagreed and dared me to prove him wrong.

Norwayne was different from other agents in the respect that he never asked me for any cash, at least not until he had gotten me a few jobs and rightfully deserved his cut.

I found modeling paled in comparison to singing with the band, but I was thankful to be making some money outside of dancing. Each day I would head out to auditions and go-sees, mostly to no avail, although I did land a bit part on television as a topless extra, as well as several other odd jobs. I even did a shoot for the government.

It was an aids awareness poster, which consequently I was mocked for by friends and acquaintances for years.

As long as I got paid though, things like that never bothered me.

My big modeling opportunity came when Norwayne sent my photos to the Wilhelmina agency in New York and they loved them.

They arranged to put me up in Manhattan for two weeks at a shared modeling house. At the time, I was still using heroin pretty heavily. Norwayne remained blissfully ignorant of my affliction. When I went to sign up for a methadone treatment program, I was rejected due to my frequent travel schedule. That meant that I was either going to have to suffer though sickness upon my arrival or bring my own drug supply. I chose the latter of the two and decided to take my chances.

However, I would only be able to safely carry and conceal enough smack for a few days and so I desperately hoped that I would find a connection while working in Manhattan.

I took the ten hour train ride from Toronto to New York and arrived in the middle of the night. As soon as I got to the agency apartment I was on the phone with friends trying to score some dope. Unfortunately I was only able to find cocaine and weed, although my hopeless search continued for the remainder of the trip. I knew it would only be a matter of time before the familiar sickness of withdrawal started to sink in and I was dreading it.

The next morning I was woken by the sounds of the other girls getting ready. There were three of them and each one seemed even more square and stupid than the next. It took me no time to realize that I had absolutely nothing in common with them and even though I intimidated them, they did their best to make me feel awkward in their space.

At eight o'clock I took the subway to the agency to check in, only to discover that I was already in trouble.

My reputation had preceded me yet again.

"There's no smoking in the apartment", said my straight faced booking agent. I knew right then that the girls were total rats and not to be trusted.

Wow, What a warm welcome, I thought to myself. They looked me up and down meticulously, recorded my measurements and took a Polaroid which was then pinned to the wall along with hundreds of others. I took a quick glance at some of the other photos and was surprised at how unattractive and unfashionable the majority of the girls were. Without a stylist to fix them up, they wouldn't be looked at twice on the street. My agent handed me my insanely busy schedule and I was glad to make my exit.

The first few days flew by in a whirlwind of photo shoots and go-sees. Every single male photographer I met turned out to be a total pervert. Each one in turn would tell me to get naked and then label me an amateur when I refused. Then they would stubbornly pout through the rest of the shoot and before I'd leave they'd ask me out on a date. Even though I was a stripper and accustomed to being naked in public, they always managed to find a way to make it feel gross and uncomfortable.

It was painfully clear why these men had gotten into the business and I found myself sympathizing with other younger, less confident models. From guilt trips, to insults, to the silent treatment, each day I encountered an entirely new manipulative approach, as each creep had perfected his own style. By the end of the week it was obvious that several of them had complained to the agency about my alleged sexual prudeness because they then booked me a supervised session to shoot some nudes. It was still icky.

While I had always attempted to integrate rock n' roll and modeling, the two jobs turned out to be drastically different in every way. There's just no personality in modeling. All they wanted me to do was keep quiet and take orders, (two things at which I have never excelled). Originality was not appreciated, self-expression was discouraged and each word spoken was one too many. In fact, every day that I was with Wilhelmina I got a little more disappointed and felt a lot more alienated. Once again things were not working out as well as I had hoped.

My second week of work had barely begun when the sickness started to sink its ugly claws in and I started to question whether or not it was all worth it.

Despite my severe discomfort I dragged myself out of bed each morning in an attempt for fulfill my obligations. I was in really rough shape and to ease the pain I began drinking heavily and snorting large amounts of blow.

Although this compensation kept me moving, I was in no shape to be running around being photographed in the New York winter.

At night I hit the strip clubs in search of smack but was unable to find a fellow user. In my desperation I ended up making the mistake of asking one of my photographers if he knew of anyone.

He seemed cool enough at the time and had joined me in drinking some shots of JD and smoking substandard American weed. Unfortunately, when it inevitably got back to the agency that I had been on the hunt for heroin I was immediately dropped.

It wasn't until a few months later that I saw the film "Gia" (a movie about a Wilhelmina supermodel who became a heroin addict, died of aids and tainted the respectability of the entire company), and realized how colossally wrong my judgment had been.

29
Some People Just Don't Last

Serious drug dealers never last long. At least the reliable ones that are worthy of financial support.

It's a ridiculously high risk job, which is why, along with my unending appetite for self destruction (I'd exhaust my own supply); I've never taken on the role of a dealer.

I do, however, possess the disturbingly canine ability to sniff one out of a crowd, bewitch them, and proceed to run up ridiculous debts.

This is one of the reasons why it's a good thing that their presence is fleeting at best.

Of all my horrendous drug tabs, there was one in particular that got completely out of control.

It was only by chance that I was relieved from it, sort of a serendipitous slap in the face.

At the time of this story, I was 24. Stacey and I were sharing a fabulous one room basement apartment near the corner of Queen and Bathurst in Toronto.

I was at the height of my heroin addiction, shooting between two to five hundred dollars a day.

I was fixing as fast as a chain smoker and therefore spent the majority of my time at the Zanzibar, trying to strip despite the bruises and the long gloves I had to wear to cover my track marks.

However, as with all junkies, no matter how much cash I made, it was never enough to be comfortable. There was the constant panic in the back of my mind wondering, How will I get through tomorrow? Where is my next fix coming from? Or How many hours left before I start getting sick?

Those thoughts never stopped. My addiction became what my life revolved around.

There was one other girl hustling at the Zanz that shared my affliction. Like me, she was bi-sexual and beautiful.

Her delicate feminine features were like those of a pixie and I found her short tomboy haircut irresistible.

She worked under the stage name Brandy and I never bothered to ask her different.

Our isolation brought us together and before long we were best friends.

It is extremely rare for an addict to share a good connection because there is always the dark possibility of a drug drought. Nevertheless, after making a couple runs together, Brandy introduced me to her guy Andy.

For some reason every heroin dealer I've ever met has been oriental. I'm not stereotyping, it's just the way it is on the streets. Orientals sell smack, Blacks push crack.

I've often thought that one of the major reasons a guy would want to get into the drug trade is the women, the desperate women to be specific.

Why else would they allow themselves to be charmed into such horrendous loans? As for Andy, I knew he liked me from the start.

Almost overnight, Andy became my sole supplier. He was the first person I'd call in the morning. We'd hang out sporadically throughout the day and then most nights he'd drive me to and from work. If I made money it went straight to him.

Andy became a regular fixture in the basement, and of course, Stacey appreciated his constant company.

As a result of our habit and the financial strain, Stacey and I started fighting much more often and became increasingly selfish and cruel to each other.

The harder we fought, the more drugs we did. Heroin completely robbed us of our sex drives, so in addition to the rage, it had been over a year since we had made love.

Together we had thrown away any intimate connection that we had once been so committed to.

As the tension in the apartment mounted, I started staying with Brandy overnight.

She had a small flat on the Yonge St. strip that was only a few doors down from the club.

She welcomed me with open arms and we had fun, at first.

We shared everything but needles and before long, she was asking me to leave Stacey and move in with her permanently. I made the decision then, to go back home. Despite it all, I was still in love with Stacey.

After that, Brandy began to distance herself from me. Although it was never my intention, I had rejected her.

The following week I was dead broke and getting sick. I called Andy and he agreed to come pick me up.

After spotting me several bags, which I injected immediately, he cut me off for the first time.

He told me that my debt had reached over $2500 and unless I showed him some major cash, I was in for the withdrawal of a lifetime.

The private discussion that followed has forever forged its place in my mind as my definitive rock bottom and it is the closest I ever came to prostitution.

I handed Andy a pair of diamond earrings that one of my regular clients had given me for Christmas the previous month.

Andy agreed to knock $500 of my tab and leave me with enough junk to function for the next two days.

If in that time, I still had no money, I would have to go to his house and work for my drugs. I spent the next couple days close to comatose, wandering around the bar like a zombie.

I knew that whatever money I did manage to make, wouldn't be enough anyway.

When the time came, and the sickness started to sink in again, I fought it as long as I could.

I had cast myself into hell and was now burning alive with the knowledge that I deserved it all.

Within hours I found myself reaching for the phone. The strange thing is, for the first time, he didn't answer.

I ended up phoning my parents and pleading with them for a loan.

Thankfully, they agreed to wire me some funds, providing this was the first and last time that I ask them for money.

By the time I scored off another connection and was stable enough to go back to work, Andy was still M.I.A.

I first heard about it on the news and it took several days for me to get the full story.

Andy had been violently stabbed several times in the neck by Brandy and one of her boyfriends during a botched drug deal.

He died in his own kitchen, covered in gushing blood.

When the cops picked up Brandy and G, she had somehow convinced him to take the full rap.

He went to jail in exchange for her freedom.

The last time I saw her she was laughing about it.

About a year later, Brandy left an urgent message on my machine, but I never phoned her back.

People like that just don't last.

30
Death is Romantic

I've always though that the most romantic thing a person can do is die. It's so extreme and tragically final. Death has made martyrs, saints and legends. It can inspire respect, credibility and compassion.

Almost all of my idols have passed on prematurely. Jim Morrison, Janis Joplin, Sid Vicious, Johnny Thunders, Wendy O'Williams Kurt Cobain, and the list goes on. By the age of twenty-six I'd already had more close friends perish than I could count on both hands.

I firmly believe that any life worth living is worth living on the edge with no fear or regrets.

People are deeply affected by death regardless of their level of personal involvement.

Someone who ordinarily may not get a second look will receive a river of tears upon their demise.

Have you ever noticed that when someone passes, everyone else claims to be so much closer to them than they actually were in life? I found this shamelessly obvious in both high school among immature minors seeking attention and sympathy at the expense of another's memory, and in fame, for pretty much the same reason.

There are few things worse than not wanting to be alive and many things worse than death. I can remember having fantasies of suicide as young as thirteen. I'd walk home from school and linger on the highway bridge debating whether or not the jump would be enough to kill me, or merely break my legs. It wasn't until I reached the age of twenty-six that I gave suicide a wholehearted and committed try.

I was living back at home with my parents going to University and trying to straighten out my life. I had just come out of a turbulent relationship with Stacy and I felt like I was getting nowhere with my band, or at least not getting far enough.

I found myself in the depths of yet another severe depression. I swallowed an entire case (15,000 mg.) of an antipsychotic drug called seroquel, chased it with a weeks worth of methadone and completed the concoction with thirty pills of an antidepressant called doxepin. It was my own recipe for fatality.

I even left a note that night. Scribbled in black ink were the words, I'm Sorry It Had To Be This Way. If I had thought that there would have been the slightest chance that I might have survived, I wouldn't have been so damn melodramatic. How mortifying. I couldn't even kill myself properly. Failed suicides are the worst sort.

After I had saturated myself with drugs, my parents found me passed out, convulsing and foaming at the mouth. The events that followed were a blur at best.

I can remember trying to talk to a team of paramedics that I couldn't understand and adamantly refusing to go to the hospital. It wasn't until the cops and the fire department showed up that there were enough of them to take me down. I put up the fight of a lifetime and it took five grown men to put me in a straight jacket, strap me to the gurney and get me in the ambulance.

I was held at the hospital for a full week and was incoherent the entire time. I found out later that they had to give me a blood transfusion to dilute the massive amounts of medication.

Believe it or not, everything that I took that night had been given to me by my doctors. Why they gave such large quantities of strong sedatives to a suicidal manic-depressive drug addict is totally beyond me. Not only that, but for months following the overdose I repeatedly made requests for some type of psychiatric help. Needless to say, I never got it.

I wish that I could tell you that things got better after that, but of course they rarely do.

Nobody seemed to care what I had done.

Plenty of people told me that they loved me, but I could never feel it. I couldn't understand how I had survived and wondered for the first time if maybe my life might be out of my hands.

The one thing about suicide is that it makes you fearless. It is literally having nothing left to lose.

That was the gift of the experience and above all else, that is what has stayed with me.

Epilogue

Compiling these tales of misguided youth was exhausting, exasperating and many times overwhelming. However, it was also extremely rewarding.

Life is never easy.

A long time ago I made the personal commitment to never have any regrets.

I believe that this can be possible, providing that you learn from your own mistakes.

Subsequently, I've learned a lot of things the hard way. Don't be afraid to live your life and to do what makes you happy.

Mistakes breed maturity and it is our experience that makes us each unique.

CJ's Songbook
Lyrics reflecting on the singer's life

All For You

I was addicted to your love
I was the rig you were my drug
I stripped my soul straight to the core
But you're not worth it anymore
Can't Stop – keep coming back to you
Can't Stand – the crap you put me through
Can't Say – the things I know I should
But I tried – I gave you all I could

I did everything that you wanted to
- But what about all the things that you kept from me
I did everything that you asked too
- Baby can't you see that it's the way you treated me
(Where the hell were you when I needed you?)
(- I had to leave to save my sanity)
You knew I did it all for you

So I'm giving up I'm moving on
Cause I've been too down for way too long
I tore it up and threw it away
There's nothing left for me to say
I Starve – myself to shrink away
I Slice – my skin to dull the pain
I'm sick - with my own sweet decay
I Know – that I'll never be the same

Backdoor Tease

Sinking down through the bloodshot crowd
Screaming at me without a sound
Keep your back up against the wall
Cause I'm creeping up quick like a cannonball

I can't believe you thought that you could punish me
I'm living as low as I'm ever gonna be
Staying out late killing every cheap fantasy
You'll never take away my luxury in poverty

It's not enough that you've got me in chains
It's not enough that you drove me insane
Skipping out like a backdoor tease
You left me crawling here on my knees

A slow and painless suicide
Stealing everything that I'm denied
Start a riot let me show you mine
Steal a kiss and walk the line
Cause I'm primed and I'm raw and I feel just right
Need a little bit of action that will do me just fine
Push me once push me twice
Shed a little bit of blood on a hot summer night

Blame Me

Strung out, set on self destruct
I've lost control and screwed it up
But what didn't kill me made me tough
Got nothing left but my bad luck

No loyalty, no sympathy
This world built up surrounding me
My old war wounds are black and blue
My track marks open up to you
There's nothing left for you to take
I can't escape, I'm suffocating here
You can blame it all on me
I've gone crazy and I've wrecked everything

I am my own worst enemy
I lose control without reasoning
I'll take you down, I'll make you bleed
I've got nothing left but my disease

Dirty Girl

Gotta feeling she's achin'
On the town, she's dolled up like a whore
Gotta feeling she's sinking
Smash down, she's swollen and she's sore

Gotta feeling she's slipping
Out cold, blacked out on the bathroom floor
Head spinning, walls dripping
She stands up and comes begging for more

Bite my tongue
The dirty deed's done
Kiss cold numb
Dirty girl common

Lips numb, black tongue baby
Dirty little girl out looking for fun
Spread wide, skin tight sweetie
Dirty little girl gonna feel alright

Down and out she's screaming
Out loud, but still can't say a word
Out of touch she's dreaming
Deep down, like she never has before

Fire In Me

This feeling, I'm falling, I'm lost in my own lunacy
I'm running, Still waiting, For you to take a piece of me
I am the bruise that never fades
I am the pill too big to take
I am the sun that cries for shade
I am the pain in your heartbreak

I'm a crazy girl, I'm out of control
Venom on my lips and a fire in my soul
I'm a crazy girl, I'm out of control
Cause I've got this fire in my soul

I'm smoking, I'm chocking, I'm looking for a fight tonight
I'm pacing, Pulse racing, I scream and bleed, I scratch and bite
I am the words you can't take back
I am the test you couldn't pass
I am the light that's fading fast
I am the love that didn't last

I'm hurting, I'm burning, My scars grow deeper by the day
I'm shaking, I'm breaking, I never wanted it this way
I am the pounding of your fist
I am the drug you can't resist
I am the liquor in the mix
I am the girl you'll never kiss

Gutter Dolls

I met her just before she died
Before the night she got too high
And she never asked me for anything
And she never said goodbye

I've been locked in here for way too long - I'm going down
I've been pushed aside for way too long – I'm going down
I've been wasting here for way too long – I'm going down
Down here in the gutters with the dead dolls

I met her best friend at the bar
Down on her knees for a little cash
She found a dead dolls severed arm
When she was looking in her trash

Hammer Down

Gotta deadline life gonna crash and burn
Got nerves of steel gonna take my turn
Time to beat myself from the inside out
Time to give it all now gonna make 'em learn

Burning black nights on the soft hot streets
Cocaine in my brain and leather on my feet
Feel my pulse and I bite my tongue
With a knife in my hand your ends just begun
If you believe in nothing anything will work
Wear your body worn and ragged
Drag your brains in the dirt
Cause I think I touched heaven but it cast me right down
Wrong time wrong place now your troubles compound

Gotta deadline life got my wheels on fire
Got the devil on my back tearing up your town
Time of no return leave it all behind
Got the engine roaring with the hammer down

Gotta deadline life on the road to hell
Started burning both ends and it's just as well
Time to spill your blood I'm not afraid to die
Gonna keep it real got no soul left to sell

In the City

Hard rock, low shot, I shock and twitch
Paranoid, dead alive, I scratch the itch
Speak out; talk loud, nothing left to say
Sharp sting, sweet pain, take me away

Empty TV screens, dirty magazines
Cheap crank and speed my only company
Bad memories of my slow deceit
Set me free from my misery (agony)

Not afraid to die a little faster
I've become a fabulous disaster
I can get it but nothing comes for free
And I still need something to believe

Spoiled rotten, hard drug fiends
Prostituting last year's beauty queens
In the city, I've seen it all and
everything that's in-between.

Kandy Koated

Sex for sale, old and stale
Drunk on scotch and ginger ale
Speed attack, feel the wrath
Riding too fast in a pitch black Cadillac

Hold on tight, break the night
Gaining on the devil, I've got him in my sights
Pistol down, dark underground
Burning up the pavement I'm better lost than found

Stiletto heels and red leather
Lipstick stains gonna bleed together
Coming at ya, kandy koated killers gonna get you cocked and loaded

Shake me, break me, living dead
Nasty little thought come spinning through my head
Beat me down ya, whip me right
Kandy koated killer come on now take a bite

Lonestar

The record skips a beat when he walks in
With a backbreakin' heartachin' sinister grin
He's a lonestar lover with a cheating heart
And he's playing like a demon gonna rip 'em apart

It's been hard for ya baby but it only gets worse
Gotta suck it back gotta quench your thirst
Gotta push yourself harder till you fall down gasping
On the floor wanting more but it's never lasting

Downtown runaround street cowboy
Like a dirty little harlot with a new sex toy
Cast a voodoo spell with a fire in his eyes
Laying down in the dirt looking up at the sky

He's looking like liquor and cigarettes
Got a chip on his shoulder with no regrets
He's been feeling weak he's been feeling old
Got the same damn story that will never be told

Lone – Star – Midnight cowboy gone too far

Lovesick

Medicated, still can't settle down
Manipulated, strong on shaken ground
Flattery has disconnected me
Shameless tease, hot, bloodthirsty

Frustrated, I degenerate
Forsaken, strive to dominate
Vicious derelict, so sadistic
Struggle dizzy, trembling, cruel, lovesick

Bittersweet, fall back on my feet
I've been around but I still can't be beat
Shot down, lovesick, losing sleep
Bone dry but crazy lovesick

Abandon fearless misery
Ferocious, spineless vanity
Lovesick, fresh wounds festering
So sore that I can't feel a thing

Deadly habit, here to pull me through
I'm reckless, help to poison you
Self indulgent, high anxiety
Sabotage my crippled sanity

Out Of Control

When the sun goes down the itch begins
Like I've got a little demon crawling under my skin
I start to twist and shake and masturbate
I've gotta swing my hips and lick my lips
But I only lose my self control
When I hear that sweet old rock n' roll

The nights still young I'm looking to find
Something that's gonna ease my state of mind
Strutted around scored a shot and a line
Five minutes later I'm feeling just fine
But I only lose my self control
When I hear that sweet old rock n' roll

The lights they burn when midnight turns
The bodies fall and rise and seethe and churn
And the music hits like a ton of bricks
Sweat stings my eyes cause I've found my fix
Said I really lost my self control
When I heard that sweet old rock n' roll

Piece Of Me

Head no warning hidden stare
Scratch me tender if you dare
I've got welts, their deeper still
I've been saving up my hate just for you

So come and get it pretty one
I'll bash your face until there's none
You can run but you can't hide
Cause I've got hell's fire on my side

Slick you slither, buy him in
Remind him how alone you've been
Keep him too high to realize
Expensive, innocent disguise

Come share a little piece of me
Taste my insanity
Smash you down, got you gagged and bound
Broken screaming on the ground

Hey cheap suit city boy
Try and take me on tonight
Try to steal just one cheap thrill
Clench your sweaty wad of bills.

Rock n' Rail

It numbs my mouth like Novocain
That little bitch she's my crack cocaine
I get the itch that I need to scratch
So I bake myself up another batch

I get off on, I get off on my,
On my Rock n' Rails

I'm over-worked and I'm under-paid
Been way too long since I've got laid
I need a fix and I need it fast
So I set myself up another blast

I get that craving that I just can't fight
To pass the day suckin' on that pipe
Cooking up class with my spoon and knife
I rock it all day and rail all night!

Shallow Dive

Had more than my share of love and drug affairs
Sold my soul, abandoned desperate prayers
Fell through fool's paradise
But beat the rap and baby I'll cheat the price

Front row, peep show, my shallow dive
Bide my time, I'm buried alive
Sore throat, tight rope, been nothing new
Out of your reach, never needed you

Bitter drip I cruise through my trip
Chest pains I've slowly gone insane
Cold sweat nothing left here to reject
Regrets I've taken down the best

Skin Deep

Brain dead, dark and empty head
Blind words, leave the rest unsaid
Heartbreak, my beautiful mistake
Bad blood starts to circulate

Tie me down I'm a mental case
Spit my love back in my face
Skin deep, it eats away at me
Break down, my common casualty

You think I've got it all but you don't know what's going on inside of me

Now I've been frozen from within
I sweat out my sweetest sin
I just can't break this ball and chain
I just can't clean my setting stain

Lift me up, throw me away
Take me home, watch me decay
Skin deep, my habits humble me
My self inflicted tragedy.

Slave to the Trade

Ya, well you're a slave to the trade
And you're living it up but it cuts
Just like a double edge blade
Drinking on the roof since a quarter to noon
Bare ass in the sun, too much too soon
Gonna kill you're time, it's a matter of mind
Kick back, six pack, relax unwind

Stick to me my sweet shock therapy
My decadent cheap fantasy
Crazy strip club casualty
You're a slave to the trade
Learn to love your ball and chain

Ya, you think you're safe from me?
Locked up, lifeless, reject refugee
Well I'm speeding down your dead end street
And I'm all dolled up for your trick or treat
Gonna live it rough, gotta soak it up
Cause too much is never enough

Stillborn

Sitting here wondering what am I living for
When all the games we used to play are nothing but a bore
I don't want to grow up to be some mindless slave
Buying into all your fake morals with the promise I'll be saved
Those hypocrites condemned my soul the day of my first screams
They should have told me long ago that nothing's as it seems
I reject your institutes and I reject your schools
I don't want to grow up to be some brainwashed fool

Sitting here all alone in this messed up place
With broken homes and broken dreams where broken people waste
I don't want to grow up and take my place in line
Numb my brain and sell my soul a little at time
I'm giving up on candy floss and cheap sideshow tricks
There's nothing left in this old world that gives me any kicks
I reject your mind control and I reject your lies
I can't live in dirty streets under your filthy skies

Won't waste my life working for the industry
And I can't put my faith in a God I'll never see
And I don't pledge my love to your tainted country
And I'll never be a part of your sick society

5 – 0

Fascist dictators of slavery
Who enforce the laws and condemn the free
You suppress my life and feed my rage
Keep stoking that fire burning inside of me

Bullies with a badge looking for a fight
With their bellies fat and their asses tight
Wanna be the man wanna take you down
Cause the man with the gun is the man with the rights

See the lights flashing in the rearview mirror
And the panic sets in with an ingrained fear
Hit the gas take the jump when there's nothing to lose
Get your finger on the trigger time to break all their rules

Government stooges with their pepper spray
Gonna clean up the streets gonna put you away
Try to take your life 'till the day you die
Time to break their rules time to make them pay

The Best It Gets

I've got a big bad attitude
And it's time to take it out on you
This feeling that I can't shake
I've had all that I can take from you
Deep inside I'm black and blue
So baby don't forget
I'm the best it gets for you

So what time did it slip your mind?
That I'm one of a kind
Your words have broke my bones
See how you feel when you're alone
So I say bye-bye, I say so long
Cause baby you know that you did me wrong

You'll never find a girl like me again
You'll never forgive yourself my friend
You're gonna learn the meaning of regret
You won't forget I'm the best it gets

You'll never find a girl like me again
You're never gonna come back in the end
Never gonna forget I'm the best it gets.

Manor House Publishing Inc.
452 Cottingham Crescent,
Ancaster, Ont., L9G 3V6
www.manor-house.biz
905-648-2193

www.ingramcontent.com/pod-product-compliance
Lightning Source LLC
Chambersburg PA
CBHW031253290426
44109CB00012B/565